heavenly desserts

DREAMY DISHES FOR EVERY OCCASION

Consultant Editor: LINDA FRASER

LORENZ BOOKS

This edition first published by Lorenz Books
an imprint of
Anness Publishing Limited
Hermes House
88–89 Blackfriars Road
London SE1 8HA

www.lorenzbooks.com

This edition distributed in Canada by Raincoast Books
8680 Cambie Street, Vancouver, British Columbia V6P 6M9

A CIP catalogue record for this book is available from the British Library

Publisher: Joanna Lorenz
Senior Cookery Editor: Linda Fraser
Designers: Tony Paine and Roy Prescott
Photographers: Steven Baxter, Karl Adamson and Amanda Heywood
Food for Photography: Wendy Lee, Jane Stevenson, Elizabeth Wolf-Cohen
Props Stylists: Blake Minton and Kirsty Rawlings
Additional recipes: Carla Capalbo and Laura Washburn

Front cover: William Lingwood, Photographer;
Helen Trent, Stylist; Sunil Vijayakar, Home Economist

Previously published as part of the *Creative Cooking Library: Dream Desserts*

1 3 5 7 9 10 8 6 4 2

MEASUREMENTS
For all recipes, quantities are given in both metric and imperial measures and,
where appropriate, measures are also given in standard cups and spoons. Follow
one set, but not a mixture because they are not interchangeable.

Standard spoon and cup measures are level.
1 tsp = 5ml, 1 tbsp = 15ml, 1 cup = 250ml/8fl oz

Australian standard tablespoons are 20ml. Australian readers should use
3 tsp in place of 1 tbsp for measuring small quantities of
gelatine, cornflour, salt etc.

Medium eggs should be used unless otherwise stated.

 The apple symbol indicates a low fat, low cholesterol recipe.

CONTENTS

INTRODUCTION

Desserts are often an indulgence, deliciously rich concoctions served at the end of a special meal. Yet they can be light and healthy, too, or simply a flavourful filler to round off a mid-week meal. When you choose a dessert it must complement the other courses. For instance, if the main course is very rich, choose a light or fruity dessert to balance it, or if the starter contains pastry, avoid this for the dessert. The time you have available to prepare will also affect your choice.

Many desserts can be made a day or two in advance others can be started early in the day and finished of just before you eat, while frozen desserts and ice cream can be made weeks in advance ready to defrost when you need them. Read the recipe through before you start so that you understand the steps involved. There are hints and tips throughout the book to help you, and in this introductory section we highlight some simple preparation tips and techniques.

MELTING CHOCOLATE

If chocolate is overheated, it can burn or develop a grainy texture, so care must be taken when melting it. If the chocolate is being melted with butter or a large quantity of liquid, this can be done in a heavy-based pan over moderately low heat. When melting chocolate alone heat it gently over hot water. Do not allow steam or any drops of water to touch the chocolate as it melts.

1 Put the chopped chocolate in a double saucepan or a bowl set over a saucepan of almost simmering water. The base should not touch the water.

2 Heat gently until the chocolate is melted and smooth, stirring occasionally. Remove from the heat.

PREPARING NUTS

1 **To skin whole almonds and pistachios**: blanch in boiling water for 2 minutes. Drain and cool slightly, then squeeze each nut to remove skins.

2 **To skin hazelnuts and brazils**: toast in a 350°F/180°C/Gas 4 oven for 10–15 minutes, then rub the nuts in a tea towel to remove the skins.

3 **To oven-toast or grill nuts**: spread nuts on a baking sheet. Toast in a 350°F/180°C/Gas 4 oven or under grill, until golden. Stir occasionally.

4 **To fry-toast nuts**: put the nuts in a frying pan, with no fat. Toast over a moderate heat until golden brown. Stir constantly.

5 **To grind nuts**: using a nut mill or coffee grinder, grind a small batch at a time. Do this carefully, if overworked, they will turn to a paste.

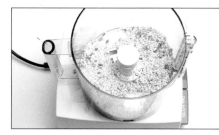

6 You can also grind nuts in a food processor. To prevent overworking the nuts grind them with some of the sugar or flour called for in the recipe.

PREPARING FRESH FRUIT

Citrus fruit

To peel completely, cut a slice from the top and from the base. Set the fruit base down on a work surface. Using a small sharp knife, cut off the peel lengthways in thick strips. Remove the coloured rind and all the white pith, which has a bitter taste. Cut following the curve of the fruit.

To remove the rind, use a vegetable peeler to shave off the rind in wide strips, taking none of the white pith. Use these strips whole or cut them into fine shreds with a sharp knife, according to recipe directions. Or rub the fruit against the fine holes of a metal grater, turning the fruit so you take just the coloured rind and not the white pith. Or use a special tool, called a citrus zester, to peel off fine threads of rind.

For slices, using a serrated knife, cut the fruit across into neat slices.

For segments, hold the peeled fruit in your cupped palm, over a bowl to catch the juice. Working from the side of the fruit to the centre, slide the knife down one side of that segment to free it from the membrane there. Drop the segment into the bowl. Continue cutting out the segments, folding back the membrane like the pages of a book as you work. When all the segments have been cut out, squeeze all the juice from the membrane.

CORING AND STONING OR SEEDING FRUIT

Apples and pears

For whole fruit, use an apple corer to stamp out the whole core.

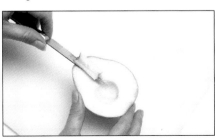

For halves, use a melon baller to scoop out the core. Cut out the stalk and base with a small sharp knife.
For quarters, cut out the stalk and core with a serrated knife.

Peaches, apricots, nectarines, plums

Cut the fruit in half, cutting round the indentation. Twist the halves apart. Lift out the stone, or lever it out with the tip of a sharp knife.

Mangoes

Cut lengthways on either side of the large flat stone in the centre. Curve the cut slightly to follow the shape of the stone. Also cut the flesh from the two thin ends of the stone.

Keeping fresh colour

If exposed to the air for long, the cut flesh of some fruits starts to turn brown. Those with a tendency to brown include apples, bananas, peaches and pears. So if prepared fruit has to wait before being served or cooked, sprinkle the cut surfaces with lemon juice. Or you can immerse hard fruits in water and lemon juice, but do not soak or the fruit may become soggy.

Pies, Tarts and Cobblers

Crisp pastry packed with fruit or a sweet filling makes a delicious dessert for any occasion – whether you want a special recipe for a dinner party or something more substantial to follow a mid-week main course. Traditional favourites with a simple pastry crust are good at any time – and those with a marshmallowy meringue topping are particularly tasty. For family meals on cooler days, choose a warming cobbler, or go for the toffee-flavoured Boston Banoffee Pie. In the summer, enclose seasonal fruits in a crumbly double crust, or show off the fruits' vibrant colours by topping the tart with a pretty lattice or a scattering of pastry shapes. For a special occasion, fresh cherries are delicious cooked under crunchy shortbread, while Lemon and Orange Tart is an elegant dessert made with winter citrus fruits.

Apple Meringue Tart

Like pears, quinces substitute well in most apple recipes. If you ever find any quinces, this is the ideal tart to use them in.

INGREDIENTS

Serves 6

50g/2oz/½ cup plain flour, sifted
75g/3oz/¾ cup wholemeal flour, sifted
pinch of salt
115g/4oz/½ cup caster sugar
75g/3oz/6 tbsp butter
1 egg, separated, plus 1 egg white
675g/1½lb eating apples
juice of ½ lemon
25g/1oz/2 tbsp butter
50g/2oz/3 tbsp demerara sugar

1 To make the pastry, sift the flours into a bowl with the salt, adding in the wheat flakes from the sieve. Add 15ml/1 tbsp of the caster sugar and rub in the butter until the mixture resembles breadcrumbs.

2 Work in the egg yolk and, if necessary, 15–30ml/1–2 tbsp cold water. Knead lightly to bring together, wrap in clear film and chill for 10–20 minutes.

3 Preheat the oven to 190°C/375°F/ Gas 5. Roll out the pastry to a 23cm/9in round and use to line a 20cm/8in flan tin. Line with grease-proof paper and fill with baking beans.

4 Bake blind for 15 minutes, then remove the paper and beans and cook for a further 5–10 minutes, until the pastry is crisp.

5 Meanwhile, peel, core and slice the apples, then toss in lemon juice. Melt the butter, add the demerara sugar and fry the apple until golden and just tender. Arrange in the pastry case.

6 Preheat the oven to 220°C/425°F/ Gas 7. Whisk the egg whites until stiff. Whisk in half the remaining caster sugar, then fold in the rest. Pipe over the apples. Bake for 6–7 minutes. Serve hot or cold with cream or ice cream.

Lemon and Orange Tart

INGREDIENTS

Serves 8–10

115g/4oz/1 cup plain flour, sifted
115g/4oz/1 cup wholemeal flour
25g/1oz/3 tbsp ground hazelnuts
25g/1oz/3 tbsp icing sugar, sifted
pinch of salt
115g/4oz/½ cup sweet butter
60ml/4 tbsp lemon curd
300g/½ pint/1¼ cups whipped cream
  or fromage frais
4 oranges, peeled and thinly sliced

1 Place the flours, hazelnuts, sugar, salt and butter in a food processor and process in short bursts until the mixture resembles breadcrumbs. Add 30–45ml/2–3 tbsp cold water and process until the dough comes together.

2 Turn out on to a lightly floured surface and knead gently until smooth. Roll out and line a 25cm/10in flat tin. Be sure not to stretch the pastry and gently ease it into the corners. Chill for 20 minutes. Preheat the oven to 190°C/375°F/Gas 5.

3 Line the pastry with greaseproof paper and fill with baking beans or bread crusts. Bake blind for 15 minutes, remove the paper and continue for a further 5–10 minutes, until the pastry is crisp. Allow to cool.

4 Whisk the lemon curd into the cream or fromage frais and spread over the base of the pastry. Arrange the orange slices on top and serve at room temperature.

Snow-capped Apples

INGREDIENTS 🍎

Serves 4

4 small Bramley cooking apples
90ml/6 tbsp orange marmalade
   or jam
2 egg whites
50g/2oz/4 tbsp caster sugar

1 Preheat the oven to 180°C/350°F/ Gas 4. Core the baking apples and score through the skins around the middle with a small sharp knife.

2 Place in a wide ovenproof dish and spoon 15ml/1 tbsp marmalade into the centre of each. Cover and bake for 35–40 minutes, or until tender.

3 Whisk the egg whites in a large bowl until stiff enough to hold soft peaks. Whisk in the sugar, then fold in the remaining marmalade.

4 Spoon the meringue over the apple then return to the oven for 10–15 minutes, or until golden. Serve hot.

— COOK'S TIP —

It is important that the egg whites are stiff enough before you add the sugar – you should be able to turn the bowl upside-down and the egg whites will stay put!

Strawberry and Apple Tart

INGREDIENTS 🍎

Serves 4–6

150g/5oz/1¼ cups self-raising flour
50g/2oz/⅔ cup rolled oats
50g/2oz/4 tbsp sunflower margarine
2 tart Bramley cooking apples,
   about 450g/1lb total weight
200g/7oz/2 cups strawberries, halved
50g/2oz/4 tbsp sugar
15ml/1 tbsp cornstarch

1 Preheat the oven to 200°C/400°F/ Gas 6. Mix together the flour and oats in a large bowl and rub in the margarine evenly. Stir in just enough cold water to bind the mixture to a firm dough. Knead lightly until smooth.

2 Roll out the pastry and line a 23cm/9in loose-based flat tin. Trim the edges, prick the base and line with greaseproof paper and baking beans. Roll out the pastry trimmings and stamp out heart shapes using a cutter.

3 Bake the pastry case for 10 minutes, remove the paper and beans, and bake for 10–15 minutes, or until golden brown. Bake the hearts until golden.

4 Peel, core, and slice the apples. Place in a pan with the strawberries, sugar, and cornflour. Cover and cook gently, stirring, until the fruit is just tender. Spoon into the pastry case and decorate with pastry hearts.

— COOK'S TIP —

It is best to prepare apples just before you use them. If you do prepare them ahead, place the cut pieces in a bowl of lemony cold water to prevent them browning.

Brown Sugar Pie

INGREDIENTS

Serves 8

175g/6oz/1½ cups plain flour
pinch of salt
20g/¾oz/2 tsp caster sugar
90ml/6 tbsp cold butter
50ml/2fl oz/¼ cup or more iced water

For the filling

25g/1oz/¼ cup plain flour, sifted
215g/7½oz/1 cup soft light brown
   sugar
2.5ml/½ tsp vanilla essence
250ml/12fl oz/1½ cups single cream
40g/1½ oz/3 tbsp butter, cut into
   tiny pieces
large pinch of grated nutmeg

1 Sift the flour, salt and sugar into a bowl. Rub in the butter until the mixture resembles coarse breadcrumbs.

2 Sprinkle with the water and mix until the dough holds together. If it is too crumbly, slowly add more water, 15ml/1 tbsp at a time. Gather into a ball and flatten. Place in a sealed polythene bag and chill for at least 20 minutes.

3 Roll out the pastry to a 3mm/⅛in thickness and line a 23cm/9in pie dish or tin. Trim all around, leaving a 1cm/½in overhang. Fold it under and flute the edge. Chill for 30 minutes.

4 Preheat the oven to 220°C/425°F/ Gas 7. Line the pastry case with a piece of greaseproof paper that is 5cm/ 2in larger all around than the diameter of the dish or tin. Fill with dried beans and bake for 8–10 minutes, until the pastry has just set. Remove from the oven and carefully lift out the paper and the beans. Prick the base of the pastry case with a fork. Return to the oven and bake for 5 minutes more. Leave the pastry case to cool slightly before filling. Turn the oven down to 190°C/375°F/Gas 5.

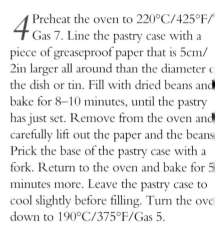

5 To make the filling, mix together the flour and sugar in a small bowl using a fork. Spread this mixture in an even layer in the base of the pastry case.

6 Stir the vanilla essence into the cream. Pour the flavoured cream over the flour and sugar mixture and gently swirl with a fork. Dot with the butter and sprinkle the nutmeg on top.

7 Cover the edge of the pie with foil strips to prevent overbrowning. Place on a baking sheet and bake for about 45 minutes, until the filling is golden brown and set to the touch. Serve the pie at room temperature.

Rhubarb Meringue Pie

INGREDIENTS

Serves 6

200g/7oz/1¾ cups plain flour
25g/1oz/½ cup ground walnuts
115g/4oz/½ cup butter, diced
275g/10oz/generous 1½ cups
  caster sugar
4 egg yolks
675g/1½lb rhubarb, cut into
  small pieces
finely grated rind and juice of 3
  blood or navel oranges
75ml/5 tbsp cornflour
3 egg whites
whipped cream, to serve

1 Sift the flour into a bowl and add the ground walnuts. Rub in the butter until the mixture resembles fine breadcrumbs. Stir in 30ml/2 tbsp of the sugar with 1 egg yolk beaten with 15ml/1 tbsp water. Mix to a firm dough. Turn out on to a floured surface and knead lightly. Wrap in a polythene bag and chill for at least 30 minutes.

2 Preheat the oven to 190°C/375°F/ Gas 5. Roll out the pastry on a lightly floured surface and use to line a 23cm/9in fluted flan tin. Prick the base with a fork. Line with greaseproof paper and fill with baking beans, then bake for 15 minutes.

3 Meanwhile, put the rhubarb, 175g/3oz/6 tbsp of the remaining sugar and the orange rind in a pan. Cover and cook over a low heat, until the rhubarb is tender.

4 Remove the beans and paper, then brush all over with a little of the remaining egg yolks. Bake for a further 10–15 minutes, until the pastry is crisp.

5 Blend the cornflour with the orange juice. Off the heat, stir the cornflour mixture into the rhubarb, then bring to the boil, stirring constantly until thickened. Cook for 1–2 minutes. Cool slightly, then beat in the remaining egg yolks. Pour into the flan case.

6 Whisk the egg whites until they form soft peaks, then whisk in the remaining sugar, 15ml/1 tbsp at a time, whisking well after each addition.

7 Swirl the meringue over the filling to cover completely. Bake for about 25 minutes until golden, then leave the pie to cool for about 30 minutes before serving with whipped cream.

Peach and Blueberry Pie

INGREDIENTS

Serves 8

225g/8oz/2 cups plain flour
pinch of salt
10ml/2 tsp sugar
150g/5oz/10 tbsp cold butter or
    margarine
1 egg yolk
50ml/2fl oz/¼ cup or more iced water
30ml/2 tbsp milk, to glaze

For the filling

450g/1lb fresh peaches, peeled, stoned
    and sliced
275g/10oz/2 cups fresh blueberries
150g/5oz/¾ cup caster sugar
30ml/2 tbsp fresh lemon juice
40g/1½oz/⅓ cup plain flour
large pinch of grated nutmeg
25g/1oz/2 tbsp butter or margarine,
    cut into tiny pieces

1 To make the pastry, sift the flour, salt and sugar into a bowl. Rub the butter or margarine into the dry ingredients as quickly as possible until the mixture resemble coarse breadcrumbs.

2 Mix the egg yolk with the iced water and sprinkle over the flour mixture. Combine with a fork until the dough holds together. If the dough is too crumbly, add a little more water, 15ml/1 tbsp at a time. Gather the dough into a ball and flatten into a round. Place in a sealed polythene bag and chill for at least 20 minutes.

3 Roll out two-thirds of the pastry between two sheets of greaseproof paper to a thickness of about 3mm/ ⅛in. Use to line a 23cm/9in pie dish. Trim all around, leaving a 1cm/½in overhang. Fold the overhang under to form the edge. Using a fork, press the edge to the rim of the pie dish or tin.

4 Gather the trimmings and remaining pastry into a ball, and roll out to a thickness of about 5mm/ ¼ in. Using a pastry wheel or sharp knife, cut into long, 1cm/½ in wide strips. Chill both the pastry case and the strips of pastry for at least 20 minutes. Meanwhile, preheat the oven to 200°C/400°F/Gas 6.

5 Line the pastry case with greaseproof paper and fill with dried beans. Bake for 7–10 minutes, until the pastry is just set. Remove from the oven and carefully lift out the paper with the beans. Prick the base of the pastry case with a fork, then return to the oven and bake for a further 5 minutes. Leave to cool slightly before filling. Leave the oven on.

6 Place the peach slices and blueberries in a bowl and stir in the sugar, lemon juice, flour and nutmeg. Spoon the fruit mixture into the pastry case. Dot the top with the pieces of butter or margarine.

7 Weave a lattice top with the chilled pastry strips, pressing the ends to the edge of the baked pastry case. Brush the strips with the milk.

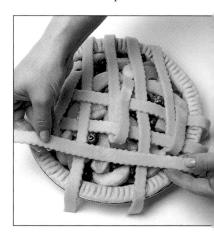

8 Bake the pie for 15 minutes. Reduce the oven temperature to 180°C/350°F/Gas 4, and continue baking for another 30 minutes, until the filling is tender and bubbling and the pastry lattice is golden. If the past becomes too brown, cover loosely with a piece of foil. Serve the pie warm or at room temperature.

— COOK'S TIP —

Don't over-chill the pastry strips. If they become too firm, they may crack and break as you weave them into a lattice.

Cherries under a Shortcake Crust

INGREDIENTS

Serves 8

450g/1lb black or red cherries, stoned
175ml/6fl oz/¾ cup grape, apple or
   cranberry juice
40g/1½oz/3 tbsp cornflour
grated rind of 1 orange
few drops vanilla essence
15–30ml/1–2 tbsp caster sugar
225g/8oz/2 cups plain flour, sifted
pinch of salt
25g/1oz/¼ cup icing sugar, sifted
225g/8oz/1 scant cup butter
60–90ml/4–6 tbsp thick cream or
   crème fraîche, to serve

1 Put the cherries in a 23cm/9in pie plate, piled high. Blend the fruit juice with 15g/½oz/1 tbsp of the cornflour, the orange rind and vanilla essence. Bring to a boil over a medium heat, stirring, until thickened. Sweeten with a little of the sugar. Leave to cool, then pour over the cherries.

2 Sift the remaining flours with the salt and icing sugar, then gently rub in the butter and, when well distributed, bring together in a ball. Or process in a food processor for a few minutes until it comes together. Knead lightly, then wrap in clear film and chill for 20 minutes.

3 Roll out the crust on a lightly floured surface, or between sheets of greaseproof paper, to the size of the top of the pie plate.

4 Preheat the oven to 180°C/350°F/ Gas 4. Brush the edge of the plate with water and carefully lift the pastry on top. Gently trim off the excess and then knock up the edges well, pressing the pastry firmly on to the rim. Flute the edge, then mark the top into eight sections and make a hole in the centre

5 Bake the pie for 20 minutes, then reduce the heat to 160°C/325°F/ Gas 3 for a further 20 minutes, until the top is golden and crisp. Sprinkle the top with caster sugar and serve hot with the cream or crème fraîche.

Upside-down Apple Tart

is delicious caramelized fruit tart
m France, known as *Tarte Tatin,*
s originally created by the Tatin
ers who ran a popular restaurant
Sologne in the Orléanais.

GREDIENTS

es 4

the pastry
/2oz/4 tbsp butter, softened
/1½oz/3 tbsp caster sugar
gg
g/4oz/1 cup plain flour
ch of salt

the apple layer
/3oz/6 tbsp butter, softened
/3oz/½ cup soft light brown
gar
Cox's Pippins apples, peeled, cored
nd thickly sliced
ipped cream, to serve

To make the pastry, cream the
butter and sugar in a bowl until
e and creamy. Beat in the egg, then
in the flour and salt and mix to a
dough. Knead lightly on a floured
face, then wrap and chill for 1 hour.

Grease a 23cm/9in cake tin then
add 50g/2oz/4 tbsp of the butter.
ce the cake tin on the hob and melt
butter gently. Remove and sprinkle
r 50g/2oz/⅓ cup of the sugar.

Arrange the apple slices on top, then
sprinkle with the remaining sugar
d dot with the remaining butter.

4 Preheat the oven to 230°C/450°F/
Gas 8. Place the cake tin on the
hob again over a low to medium heat
for about 15 minutes, until a light
golden caramel forms on the bottom.
Remove the pan from the heat.

5 Roll out the pastry on a lightly
floured surface to a round the
same size as the tin and lay on top of
the apples. Tuck the pastry edges down
round the sides of the apples.

6 Bake for about 20–25 minutes,
until the pastry is golden. Remove
the tart from the oven and leave to
stand for about 5 minutes.

7 Place an upturned plate on top of
the tin and holding the two
together with a dish towel, turn the
apple tart out on to the plate. Serve
while still warm with whipped cream.

COOK'S TIP

Cox's Pippins apples are perfect for this
tart because they hold their shape so well.
If they are not available, use another firm,
sweet eating apple instead.

Maple Cider Pie

INGREDIENTS

Serves 6

175g/6oz/1½ cups plain flour
1.25ml/¼ tsp salt
10ml/2 tsp sugar
115g/4oz/½ cup cold butter or
  margarine
50g/2fl oz/¼ cup or more iced water

For the filling

15g/½oz/1 tbsp butter
250ml/8fl oz/1 cup maple syrup
50ml/2fl oz/¼ cup water
600ml/1 pint/2½ cups cider
2 eggs, at room temperature, separated
5ml/1 tsp grated nutmeg

1 To make the pastry, sift the flour, salt and sugar into a bowl. Using a pastry blender or two knives, cut the butter or margarine into the dry ingredients as quickly as possible until the mixture resembles breadcrumbs.

2 Sprinkle the iced water over the flour mixture. Combine with a fork until the dough holds together. If the dough is too crumbly, add a little more water, 15ml/1 tbsp at a time. Gather the dough into a ball and flatten into a round. Place in a polythene bag and chill for at least 20 minutes.

3 Meanwhile, place the cider in a saucepan and boil until only 175ml/6fl oz/¾ cup remains, then cool.

4 Roll out the pastry between two sheets of greaseproof or non-stick baking paper to 3mm/⅛in thickness. Use to line a 23cm/9in pie dish.

5 Trim around the edge, leaving a 1cm/½in overhang. Fold the overhang under to form the edge. Using a fork, press the edge to the rim of the dish and press up from under with your fingers at intervals to make a ruffle effect. Chill the pastry case for at least 20 minutes. Preheat the oven to 180°C/350°F/Gas 4.

6 To make the filling, place the butter, maple syrup, water and cider in a pan and simmer gently for about 5–6 minutes. Remove the pan from the heat and leave the mixture to cool slightly, then whisk in the beaten egg yolks.

7 Whisk the egg whites in a large bowl, until they form stiff peaks. Add the cider mixture and fold gently together until evenly blended.

8 Pour the mixture into the prepared pastry case. Dust with the grated nutmeg. Bake the pie for 30–35 minutes, until the pastry is golden brown and the filling is well set and golden. Serve warm.

Strawberry and Blueberry Tart

This tart works equally well using either autumn or winter fruits as long as there is a riot of colour and the fruit is ripe.

INGREDIENTS

Serves 6–8
225g/8oz/2 cups plain flour
pinch of salt
75g/3oz/9 tbsp icing sugar
150g/5oz/10 tbsp unsalted butter, diced
1 egg yolk

For the filling
350g/12oz/1³⁄₄ cups mascarpone
30ml/2 tbsp icing sugar
few drops vanilla essence
finely grated rind of 1 orange
450–675g/1–1¹⁄₂lb fresh mixed strawberries and blueberries
90ml/6 tbsp redcurrant jelly
30ml/2 tbsp orange juice

1 Sift the flour, salt and sugar into a bowl, and rub in the butter until the mixture resembles coarse crumbs. Using a round-bladed knife, mix in the egg yolk and 10ml/2 tsp cold water. Gather the dough together, then turn out on to a floured surface and knead lightly until smooth. Wrap and chill for 1 hour.

2 Preheat the oven to 190°C/375°F/ Gas 5. Roll out the pastry and use to line a 2.5cm/10in fluted flan tin. Prick the base and chill for 15 minutes.

3 Line the chilled pastry case with greaseproof paper and baking beans, then bake for 15 minutes. Remove the paper and beans and bake for a further 15 minutes, until crisp and golden. Leave to cool in the tin.

4 Beat together the mascarpone, sugar, vanilla essence and orange rind in a mixing bowl until smooth.

5 Tip the pastry case out of the tin, then spoon in the filling and pile the fruits on top. Heat the redcurrant jelly with the orange juice until runny, sieve, then brush over the fruit to glaze.

Boston Banoffee Pie

INGREDIENTS

Makes an 20cm/8in pie

150g/5oz/1¼ cups plain flour
225g/8oz/1 cup butter
50g/2oz/4 tbsp caster sugar
2 x 405g/14oz can skimmed,
  sweetened condensed milk
115g/4oz/²⁄₃ cup soft light brown sugar
30ml/2 tbsp golden syrup
4 small bananas, sliced
a little lemon juice
whipped cream, to decorate
5ml/1 tsp grated plain chocolate

1 Preheat the oven to 160°C/325°F/
Gas 3. Place the flour and 115g/4oz/
½ cup of the butter in a food processor
and blend until crumbed (or rub in with
your fingertips). Stir in the caster sugar.

2 Squeeze the mixture together with
your hands until it forms a dough.
Press into the base of an 20cm/8in loose-
based fluted flan tin. Bake for 25–30
minutes, until lightly browned.

3 Place the remaining 115g/4oz/½
cup of butter with the condensed
milk, brown sugar and golden syrup in
a large non-stick saucepan and heat
gently, stirring, until the butter has
melted and the sugar has dissolved.

4 Bring to a gentle boil and cook
for 7 minutes, stirring all the time
(to prevent burning), until the mixture
thickens and turns a light caramel
colour. Pour on to the cooked pastry
base and leave until cold.

5 Sprinkle the bananas with lemon
juice and arrange in overlapping
circles on top of the caramel filling,
leaving a gap in the centre. Pipe a swirl
of whipped cream in the centre and
sprinkle with the grated chocolate.

Spiced Red Fruit Compôte

INGREDIENTS

Serves 4

4 ripe red plums, halved
225g/8oz/2 cups strawberries, halved
225g/8oz/1¾ cups raspberries
30ml/2 tbsp light muscovado sugar
30ml/2 tbsp cold water
1 cinnamon stick
3 pieces star anise
6 cloves

--- COOK'S TIP ---

Light muscovado sugar has a mild, treacly flavour and is delicious in this recipe. You could use soft light brown sugar, or even caster, if you prefer.

1 Place the plums, strawberries, and raspberries in a heavy-based pan with the sugar and water.

2 Add the cinnamon stick, star anise, and cloves to the pan and heat gently, without boiling, until the sugar dissolves and the fruit juices run.

3 Cover the pan and leave the fruit infuse over very low heat for abou 5 minutes. Remove the spices from th compôte before serving warm, with natural yogurt or fromage frais.

Rhubarb Spiral Cobbler

INGREDIENTS

Serves 4

675g/1½lb rhubarb, sliced
50g/2oz/4 tbsp caster sugar
45ml/3 tbsp orange juice
200g/7oz/1⅓ cups self-raising flour
30ml/2 tbsp caster sugar
about 200g/7oz/1 cup natural yogurt
grated rind of 1 medium orange
30ml/2 tbsp demerara sugar
5ml/1 tsp ground ginger

1 Preheat the oven to 200°C/400°F/ Gas 6. Cook the rhubarb, sugar, and orange juice in a covered pan until tender. Tip into an ovenproof dish.

2 To make the topping, mix the flour and caster sugar, then stir in enough of the yogurt to bind to a soft dough.

3 Roll out on a floured surface to a 25cm/10in square. Mix the orange rind, demerara sugar, and ginger, then sprinkle this over the dough.

4 Roll up quite tightly, then cut int about 10 slices using a sharp knife Arrange the slices over the rhubarb.

5 Bake in the oven for 15–20 minute or until the spirals are well risen and golden brown. Serve warm, with yogurt or custard.

--- COOK'S TIP ---

When you make the cobbler topping, mix together just enough to form a soft, not sticky dough. To keep it light, don't over-work the dough and roll out gently.

Blackberry Cobbler

INGREDIENTS

Serves 8

750g/1¾lb blackberries
200g/7oz/1 cup caster sugar, plus
   25g/1oz/2 tbsp sugar mixed with
   1.25ml/¼ tsp grated nutmeg
25g/1oz/3 tbsp plain flour
grated rind of 1 lemon

For the topping

225g/8oz/2 cups plain flour
200g/7oz/1 cup caster sugar
15ml/1 tbsp baking powder
pinch of salt
250ml/8fl oz/1 cup milk
115g/4oz/½ cup butter, melted

1 Preheat the oven to 180°C/350°F/
Gas 4. Place the blackberries, sugar,
flour and lemon rind in a large bowl.
Stir gently to coat the blackberries,
then transfer to a 1.75 litre/3 pint/
7½ cup baking dish.

2 To make the topping, sift the flour
sugar, baking powder and salt into
a large bowl and set aside. Blend the
milk and butter in a large jug.

3 Gradually pour the milk mixture
into the dry ingredients and stir
until the mixture is just smooth.

4 Spoon the mixture over the
blackberries, spreading evenly.

5 Sprinkle the surface with the sugar
and nutmeg mixture. Bake for
about 50 minutes, until the topping is
set and lightly browned. Serve hot.

Lemon Meringue Pie

INGREDIENTS

Makes a 7½in pie
115g/4oz/1 cup plain flour
50g/2oz/4 tbsp butter, diced
25g/1oz/3 tbsp ground almonds
25g/1oz/3 tbsp caster sugar
1 egg yolk

For the filling
juice of 3 lemons
finely grated rind of 2 lemons
45ml/3 tbsp cornflour
90g/3oz/6 tbsp caster sugar
2 egg yolks
15ml/1 tbsp butter

For the meringue
3 egg whites
115g/4oz/½ cup caster sugar

1 To make the pastry, sift the flour into a bowl, add the butter and rub with your fingertips until the mixture resembles breadcrumbs (or use a food processor). Stir in the ground almonds and sugar, and add the egg yolk and 30ml/2 tbsp cold water. Mix with your hands until the pastry comes together.

2 Knead lightly on a floured surface then wrap and chill for about 30 minutes. Meanwhile, preheat the oven to 200°C/400°F/Gas 6 and pop in a baking sheet to heat up.

3 Roll out the pastry to a 20cm/8in round and use it to line a 18.5cm/7½in fluted loose-based flat tin. Prick the base with a fork. Line with grease-proof paper and fill with baking beans.

4 Place the tin on the preheated baking sheet and bake blind for 12 minutes. Remove the paper and beans and bake for a further 5 minutes. Remove from the oven and cool. Reduce the temperature to 150°C/300°F/Gas 2.

5 To make the filling, put the lemon juice and rind into a jug (you should have 150ml/¼ pint/⅔ cup). Blend the cornflour with a little of the lemon juice, then gradually stir in the rest. Pour into a saucepan and add 150ml/¼ pint/⅔ cup water.

6 Bring slowly to a boil, stirring until smooth and thickened. Remove from the heat and beat in the sugar and egg yolks, then add the butter. Spoon into the pastry case.

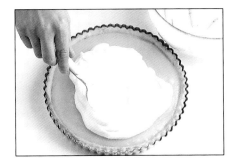

7 To make the meringue, whisk the egg whites until stiff, then gradually whisk in the sugar a tablespoon at a time until thick and glossy. Pile the meringue on top of the lemon filling, spreading and swirling it with the back of a spoon. Bake for 30–35 minutes, or until the meringue is golden and crisp.

Fresh Fruit Desserts

We think mainly of fruit desserts in the summer, yet they are excellent at any time of year. In the cooler months, serve fruits warm – pears poached in red wine make a classic dish, but try them cooked in cider for a change, or combine them with apricots and wrap in crisp layers of filo pastry. Pineapple Flambé is quick to rustle up for an impromptu dessert, and the recipe for Hot Bananas with Rum and Raisins turns an everyday fruit into an exotic delight, while Clementines in Cinnamon Caramel is quite the prettiest, simple dessert. Even in the summer, fruits can be served hot and peaches are delicious roasted with a chocolate and amaretti stuffing. But this is the time of year for cool fruits, and the Chinese or Emerald fruit salads, or Strawberries in Spiced Grape Jelly, are all fruit desserts at their refreshing best.

Summer Berry Medley

Make the most of glorious seasonal fruits in this refreshing dessert. The sauce is also good swirled into plain or strawberry-flavoured fromage frais.

INGREDIENTS

Serves 4–6
175g/6oz redcurrants
175g/6oz raspberries
50g/2oz caster sugar
30–45ml/2–3 tbsp crème de framboise
450–675g/1–1½ lb mixed soft summer
   fruits, such as strawberries,
   raspberries, blueberries, redcurrants
   and blackcurrants
vanilla ice cream, to serve

1 Strip the redcurrants from their stalks using a fork and place in a bowl with the raspberries, sugar and crème de framboise. Cover and leave to macerate for 1–2 hours.

2 Put this fruit with its macerating juices in a pan and cook gently for 5–6 minutes, stirring occasionally, until the fruit is just tender.

3 Pour the fruit into a blender or food processor and blend until smooth. Press through a nylon sieve to remove any pips. Leave to cool, then chill.

4 Divide the mixed soft fruit among four individual glass serving dishes and pour over the sauce. Serve with scoops of vanilla ice cream.

Apricot and Pear Filo Roulade

This is a very quick way of making
a strudel – normally, very time
consuming to do – it tastes delicious
all the same!

INGREDIENTS

Serves 4–6

115g/4oz/²⁄₃ cup ready-to-eat dried
  apricots, chopped
30ml/2 tbsp apricot preserve
5ml/1 tsp lemon juice
50g/2oz/¼ cup soft brown sugar
2 medium-sized pears, peeled, cored
  and chopped
50g/2oz/½ cup ground almonds
30ml/2 tbsp slivered almonds
4 sheets filo pastry
25g/1oz/2 tbsp butter, melted
icing sugar, to dust

1 Put the apricots, apricot preserve,
lemon juice, brown sugar and pears
into a pan and heat gently, stirring, for
5–7 minutes.

2 Remove from the heat and cool.
Mix in the ground and flaked
almonds. Preheat the oven to 200°C/
400°F/Gas 6. Melt the butter in a pan.

3 Lightly grease a baking sheet. Layer
the pastry on the baking sheet,
brushing each layer with butter.

4 Spoon the filling down the pastry
just to one side of the centre and
within 2.5cm/1in of each end. Lift the
other side of the pastry up by sliding a
palette knife underneath.

5 Fold this pastry over the filling,
tucking the edge under. Seal the
ends neatly and brush all over with
butter again.

6 Bake for 15–20 minutes, until
golden. Dust with icing sugar and
serve hot with cream or fromage frais.

Pineapple Flambé

Flambéing means adding alcohol and then burning it off so the flavour is not too overpowering. This recipe is just as good, however, without the brandy – perfect if you wish to serve it to young children.

INGREDIENTS

Serves 4
1 large, ripe pineapple
40g/1½oz/3 tbsp unsalted butter
40g/1½oz/3 tbsp brown sugar
60ml/4 tbsp fresh orange juice
30ml/2 tbsp brandy or vodka
25g/1oz/2 tbsp slivered almonds, toasted

1 Cut away the top and base of the pineapple. Then cut down the sides, removing all the dark 'eyes', but leaving the pineapple in a good shape.

2 Cut the pineapple into thin slices and, with an apple corer, remove the hard central core.

3 In a large frying pan melt the butter, sugar and orange juice. Add the pineapple slices and cook for about 1–2 minutes, turning once.

4 Add the brandy or vodka and light with a match immediately. Let the flames die down and then sprinkle with the almonds and serve with ice cream or thick yogurt.

Warm Pears in Cider

INGREDIENTS

Serves 4
1 lemon
50g/2oz/¼ cup caster sugar
a little grated nutmeg
250ml/8fl oz/1 cup sweet cider
4 firm, ripe pears
single cream, to serve

1 Carefully remove the rind from the lemon with a potato peeler leaving any white pith behind.

2 Squeeze the juice from the lemon into a saucepan, add the rind, sugar, nutmeg and cider and heat through to dissolve the sugar.

3 Carefully peel the pears, leaving the stalks on if possible, and place them in the pan of cider. Poach the pears for 10–15 minutes until almost tender, turning them frequently.

4 Transfer the pears to individual serving dishes using a slotted spoon. Simmer the liquid over a high heat until it reduces slightly and becomes syrupy.

5 Pour the warm syrup over the pears and serve at once with freshly made custard, cream or ice cream.

COOK'S TIP

To get pears of just the right firmness, you may have to buy them slightly under-ripe and then wait a day or more. Soft pears are no good at all for this dish.

Banana, Maple and Lime Pancakes

Pancakes are a treat any day of the week, and they can be made in advance and stored in the freezer for convenience.

INGREDIENTS 🍎

Serves 4
115g/4oz/1 cup plain flour
1 egg white
250ml/8fl oz/1 cup skimmed milk
50ml/2fl oz/¼ cup cold water
sunflower oil, for frying

For the filling
4 bananas, sliced
45ml/3 tbsp maple syrup or golden
   syrup
30ml/2 tbsp lime juice
strips of lime rind, to decorate

1 Beat together the flour, egg white, milk and water until smooth and bubbly. Chill until needed.

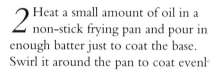

2 Heat a small amount of oil in a non-stick frying pan and pour in enough batter just to coat the base. Swirl it around the pan to coat evenl[y]

3 Cook until golden, then toss or tu[rn] and cook the other side. Place on [a] plate, cover with foil and keep hot while making the remaining crêpes.

4 To make the filling, place the bananas, syrup and lime juice in [a] pan and simmer gently for 1 minute. Spoon into the pancakes and fold into quarters. Sprinkle with shreds of lime rind to decorate. Serve hot, with yogurt or low fat fromage frais.

COOK'S TIP
Pancakes freeze well. To store for later use, interleave them with non-stick baking paper, overwrap, and freeze for up to 3 months.

VARIATION
To make Mango, Maple and Lime Pancakes, substitute two ripe, medium-sized mangoes for the bananas. Cut each mango in three around the stone, then peel and cut the flesh into thick slices.

Apple Foam with Blackberries

is lovely light dish is perfect if
u fancy a dessert, but don't want
thing too rich.

GREDIENTS 🍎

ves 4
5g/8oz blackberries
)ml/¼ pint/⅔ cup apple juice
1/1 tbsp powdered gelatine
nl/1 tbsp clear honey
gg whites

Place the blackberries in a pan with
60ml/4 tbsp of the apple juice and
t gently until the fruit is soft.
move from the heat, cool, and chill.

Sprinkle the gelatine over the
remaining apple juice in a small
and stir over low heat until
olved. Stir in the honey.

Whisk the egg whites until they
hold stiff peaks. Continue whisking
d and pour in the hot gelatine
ture gradually, until well mixed.

4 Quickly spoon the foam into
rough mounds on individual plates.
Chill. Serve with the blackberries and
juice spooned around.

COOK'S TIP

Make sure that you dissolve the gelatine
over a very low heat. It must not boil, or
it will lose its setting ability.

VARIATION

Other seasonal soft fruits, such as raspberries, strawberries, peaches or apricots, could be used in place of the blackberries, if you like.

Banana Honey Yogurt Ice

INGREDIENTS 🍎

Serves 4–6

4 ripe bananas, chopped roughly
15ml/1 tbsp lemon juice
30ml/2 tbsp clear honey
250g/9oz/1 cup Greek-style yogurt
2.5ml/½ tsp ground cinnamon
crisp biscuits, flaked hazelnuts, and
   banana slices, to serve

— VARIATION —

To make Banana Maple Yogurt Ice, use maple syrup in place of the clear honey. Check that the syrup is 100% pure, cheaper substitutes have little of the real flavour.

---

1 Place the bananas in a food processor or blender with the lemon juice, honey, yogurt, and cinnamon. Process until smooth and creamy.

2 Pour the mixture into a freezer container and freeze until almost solid. Spoon back into the food processor and process again until smooth.

3 Return to the freezer until firm. Allow to soften at room temperature for 15 minutes, then serve in scoops, with crisp biscuits, flaked hazelnuts, and banana slices.

Autumn Pudding

INGREDIENTS 🍎

Serves 6

10 slices white or brown bread, at least
   one day old
1 Bramley cooking apple, peeled, cored,
   and sliced
225g/8oz ripe red plums, halved and
   stoned
225g/8oz blackberries
60ml/4 tbsp water
75g/3oz/6 tbsp caster sugar

1 Remove the crusts from the bread and use a biscuit cutter to stamp out a 7.5cm/3in round from one slice. Cut the remaining slices in half.

2 Place the bread round in the base of a 1.2 litre/2 pint/5 cup pudding basin, then overlap the fingers around the sides, saving some for the top.

3 Place the apple, plums, blackberries, water and caster sugar in a pan, heat gently until the sugar dissolves, then simmer gently for 10 minutes, or until soft. Remove from the heat.

4 Reserve the juice and spoon the fruit into the bread-lined basin. Top with the reserved bread, then spoon over the reserved fruit juices.

5 Cover the mould with a saucer and place weights on top. Chill the puding overnight. Turn out onto serving plate and serve with low fat yogurt or fromage frais.

— COOK'S TIP —

Choose good-quality bread that is not too thinly sliced – it needs to be at least 5mm/¼in thick so that it supports the fruit when the pudding is turned out.

Clementines in Cinnamon Caramel

The combination of sweet, yet sharp clementines and caramel sauce with a hint of spice is divine. Served with Greek-style yogurt or crème fraîche, this makes a delicious dessert.

INGREDIENTS

Serves 4–6
8–12 clementines
225g/8oz/1 cup granulated sugar
2 cinnamon sticks
30ml/2 tbsp orange-flavoured liqueur
25g/1oz/¼ cup shelled pistachio nuts

1 Pare the rind from two clementines using a vegetable peeler and cut it into fine strips. Set aside.

2 Peel the clementines, removing all the pith but keeping them intact. Put the fruits in a serving bowl.

3 Gently heat the sugar in a pan until it dissolves and turns a rich golden brown. Immediately turn off the heat.

4 Cover your hand with a dish tow and pour in 300ml/½ pint/1¼ cup warm water (the mixture will bubble and splutter). Bring slowly to the boil, stirring until the caramel has dissolved. Add the shredded peel and cinnamon sticks, then simmer for 5 minutes. Stir in the orange-flavoured liqueur.

5 Leave the syrup to cool for about 10 minutes, then pour over the clementines. Cover the bowl and chill for several hours or overnight.

6 Blanch the pistachio nuts in boiling water. Drain, cool and remove the dark outer skins. Scatter over the clementines and serve at once.

Hot Bananas with Rum and Raisins

oose almost-ripe bananas with
enly coloured skins, either all
llow or just green at the tips.
ick patches indicate that the fruit
over-ripe.

GREDIENTS

ves 4

g/1½oz/¼ cup seedless raisins
ml/5 tbsp dark rum
g/2oz/4 tbsp unsalted butter
ml/4 tbsp soft light brown sugar
ipe bananas, peeled and halved
engthways
5ml/¼ tsp grated nutmeg
5ml/¼ tsp ground cinnamon
ml/2 tbsp slivered almonds, toasted
lled cream or vanilla ice cream,
o serve (optional)

Put the raisins in a bowl with the
rum. Leave them to soak for about
minutes to plump up.

Melt the butter in a frying pan,
add the sugar and stir until
solved. Add the bananas and cook
a few minutes until tender.

3 Sprinkle the spices over the
bananas, then pour over the rum
and raisins. Carefully set alight using a
long taper and stir gently to mix.

4 Scatter over the slivered almonds
and serve immediately with chilled
cream or vanilla ice cream, if you like.

Emerald Fruit Salad

INGREDIENTS 🍎

Serves 4

30ml/2 tbsp lime juice
30ml/2 tbsp clear honey
2 green eating apples, cored and sliced
1 small ripe Ogen melon, diced
2 kiwi fruit, sliced
1 star fruit, sliced
mint sprigs, to decorate

1 Mix together the lime juice and honey in a large bowl, then toss the apple slices in this.

2 Stir in the melon, kiwi fruit and star fruit. Place in a glass serving dish and chill before serving.

3 Decorate with mint sprigs and serve with yogurt or fromage fra

—— COOK'S TIP ——

Starfruit is best when fully ripe – look for plump, yellow fruit.

—— VARIATION ——

Although they might not fit the green theme, other fruits could be added to this salad – try sliced peaches, strawberries plums, bananas or pears.

Peach and Ginger Pashka

This simpler adaptation of a Russian Easter favourite is made with much lighter ingredients than the traditional version.

INGREDIENTS 🍎

Serves 4–6

350g/12oz/1½ cups low fat cottage cheese
2 ripe peaches or nectarines
90g/3½oz/⅓ cup low fat natural yogurt
2 pieces stem ginger in syrup, drained and chopped
30ml/2 tbsp stem ginger syrup
2.5ml/½ tsp vanilla essence
peach slices and toasted flaked almonds, to decorate

—— COOK'S TIP ——

Rather than making one large pashka, line four to six individual cups or ramekins with the clean cloth or muslin and divide the mixture among them.

1 Drain the cottage cheese and rub through a sieve into a bowl. Stone and roughly chop the peaches.

2 Mix together the chopped peaches, cottage cheese, yogurt, ginger, syrup, and vanilla essence.

3 Line a new, clean flower pot or strainer with a piece of clean, fin cloth such as cheesecloth.

4 Tip in the cheese mixture, then wrap over the cloth and place a weight on top. Leave over a bowl in cool place to drain overnight. To serve, unwrap the cloth and invert th pashka on to a plate. Decorate with peach slices and almonds.

Grape Cheese Whip

INGREDIENTS

Serves 4

150g/5oz/1 cup black or green
    seedless grapes, plus 4 sprigs
2 egg whites
15ml/1 tbsp caster sugar
finely grated rind and juice of ½ lemon
225g/8oz/1 cup skimmed milk soft
    cheese
45ml/3 tbsp clear honey
30ml/2 tbsp brandy

―――――― COOK'S TIP ――――――

Serve this light dessert soon after it is made
– it may begin to separate if you leave it
standing too long.

1 Brush the sprigs of grapes lightly
with egg white and sprinkle with
sugar to coat. Leave to dry.

2 Mix together the lemon rind and
juice, cheese, honey, and brandy
Chop the remaining grapes and stir in

3 Whisk the egg whites until stiff
enough to hold soft peaks. Fold
the whites into the grape mixture, the
spoon into serving glasses.

4 Top with sugar-frosted grapes an
serve chilled.

Strawberries in Spiced Grape Jelly

INGREDIENTS

Serves 4

450ml/¾ pint/1⅞ cups red grape juice
1 cinnamon stick
1 small orange
15ml/1 tbsp/1 sachet gelatine
225g/8oz strawberries, chopped
strawberries and orange rind,
    to decorate

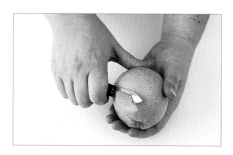

1 Place the grape juice in a pan with
the cinnamon. Thinly pare the
rind from the orange and add to the
pan. Infuse over a very low heat for 10
minutes, then remove the flavourings.

2 Squeeze the juice from the orange
and sprinkle over the gelatine. Stir
into the grape juice to dissolve. Allow
to cool until just beginning to set.

3 Stir in the strawberries and quick
tip into a 1 litre/1¾ pint/4 cup
mould or serving dish. Chill until set.

4 To turn out, dip the mould quick
into hot water and invert on to a
serving plate. Decorate with fresh
strawberries and shreds of orange rind

―――――― VARIATION ――――――

Raspberries could be used in place of all or
just some of the strawberries in this jelly. If
the raspberries are frozen, stir them into
the jelly while it is still warm, otherwise it
will set immediately.

Poached Pears in Red Wine

INGREDIENTS

Serves 4

1 bottle red wine
150g/5oz/³/₄ cup caster sugar
45ml/3 tbsp honey
juice of ½ lemon
1 cinnamon stick
1 vanilla pod, split open lengthways
5cm/2in piece of orange rind
1 clove
1 black peppercorn
4 firm, ripe pears
whipped cream or soured cream,
    to serve

1 Place the wine, sugar, honey, lemon juice, cinnamon stick, vanilla pod, orange rind, clove and peppercorn in a saucepan just large enough to hold the pears standing upright. Heat gently, stirring occasionally until the sugar has completely dissolved.

2 Meanwhile, peel the pears, leaving the stem intact. Take a thin slice off the base of each pear so that it will stand square and upright.

3 Place the pears in the wine mixture, then simmer, uncovered for 20–35 minutes depending on size and ripeness, until the pears are just tender; be careful not to overcook.

4 Carefully transfer the pears to a bowl using a slotted spoon. Continue to boil the poaching liquid until reduce by about half. Leave to cool, then strain the cooled liquid over the pears and chill for at least 3 hours.

5 Place the pears in four individual serving dishes and spoon over a little of the red wine syrup. Serve with whipped cream or soured cream.

Chocolate Amaretti Peaches

…uick and easy to prepare,
…s delicious dessert can also
… made with fresh nectarines
… apricots.

…GREDIENTS

…ves 4

…5g/4oz amaretti biscuits, crushed
…g/2oz plain chocolate, chopped
…ted rind of ½ orange
…ml/1 tbsp clear honey
…25ml/¼ tsp ground cinnamon
…gg white, lightly beaten
…irm ripe peaches
…0ml/¼ pint/⅔ cup white wine
…ml/1 tbsp caster sugar
…hipped cream, to serve

…▊ Preheat the oven to 190°C/375°F/
… Gas 5. Mix together the crushed
…aretti biscuits, chocolate, orange
…d, honey and cinnamon in a bowl.
…ld the beaten egg white and mix to
…d the mixture together.

…▊ Halve and stone the peaches and
… fill the cavities with the chocolate
…xture, mounding it up slightly.

3 Arrange the stuffed peaches in a
lightly buttered, shallow ovenproof
dish which will just hold the peaches
comfortably. Pour the wine into a
measuring cup and stir in the sugar.

4 Pour the wine mixture around the
peaches. Bake for 30–40 minutes,
until the peaches are tender. Serve at
once with a little of the cooking juices
spooned over and the whipped cream.

Creamy Mango Cheesecake

Cheesecakes are always a favourite but sadly they are often high in fat. This one is the exception.

INGREDIENTS

Serves 4
115g/4oz/1¼ cups rolled oats
40g/1½oz/3 tbsp sunflower margarine
30ml/2 tbsp clear honey
1 large ripe mango
300g/10oz/1¼ cups low fat soft cheese
150g/5oz/⅔ cup low fat natural yogurt
finely grated rind of 1 small lime
45ml/3 tbsp apple juice
20ml/4 tsp powdered gelatine
fresh mango and lime slices,
   to decorate

1 Preheat the oven to 200°C/400°F/ Gas 6. Mix together the oats, margarine and honey. Press into the base of a 20cm/8in loose-bottomed cake tin. Bake for 12–15 minutes, until lightly browned. Cool.

2 Peel, stone, and roughly chop the mango. Place the chopped mango, cheese, yogurt, and lime rind in a food processor and process until smooth.

3 Heat the apple juice until boiling, sprinkle the gelatine over it, stir to dissolve, then stir into cheese mixture.

4 Pour the cheese mixture into the tin and chill until set, then turn out on to a serving plate. Decorate the top with mango and lime slices.

--- COOK'S TIP ---

Remember to remove the apple juice from the heat before you sprinkle over the powdered gelatine – it should be hot, but not simmering or boiling.

Frudités with Honey Dip

INGREDIENTS

Serves 4
225g/8oz/1 cup Greek-style yogurt
45ml/3 tbsp clear honey
selection of fresh fruit for dipping
   such as apples, pears, tangerines,
   grapes, figs, cherries, strawberries,
   and kiwi fruit

--- COOK'S TIP ---

If you aren't going to serve the fruit as soon as it is prepared, brush any apple and pear pieces with a little lemon juice to prevent them browning.

1 Place the yogurt in a dish, beat until smooth, then stir in the honey, leaving a little marbled effect.

2 Cut the fruit into wedges or bite-sized pieces, or leave whole.

3 Arrange the fruit on a platter with the bowl of honey dip in the centre. Serve chilled.

Chinese Fruit Salad

For an unusual fruit salad with an oriental flavour, try this mixture of fruits in a tangy lime and lychee syrup topped with a light sprinkling of toasted sesame seeds.

INGREDIENTS

Serves 4
115g/4oz/½ cup caster sugar
thinly pared rind and juice of 1 lime
400g/14oz can lychees in syrup
1 ripe mango, stoned and sliced
1 eating apple, cored and sliced
2 bananas, chopped
1 star fruit, sliced (optional)
5ml/1 tsp sesame seeds, toasted

1 Place the sugar in a saucepan with 300ml/½ pint/1¼ cups water and the pared lime rind. Heat gently until the sugar dissolves, then increase the heat and boil gently for about 7–8 minutes. Remove from the heat and leave on one side to cool.

2 Drain the lychees into a jug and pour the juice into the cooled li syrup with the lime juice. Place all t prepared fruit in a bowl and pour ov the lime and lychee syrup. Chill for about 1 hour. Just before serving, sprinkle with toasted sesame seeds.

Apricot and Almond Jalousie

Jalousie means "shutter" in French, and the traditional slatted puff pastry topping of this fruit pie looks exactly like the shutters which adorn the windows of French houses.

INGREDIENTS

Serves 4
225g/8oz ready-made puff pastry
a little beaten egg
90ml/6 tbsp apricot conserve
30ml/2 tbsp caster sugar
30ml/2 tbsp flaked almonds
cream or natural yogurt, to serve

1 Preheat the oven to 220°C/425°F/ Gas 7. Roll out the pastry on a lightly floured surface and cut into a 30cm/12in square. Cut in half to make two rectangles.

2 Place one piece of pastry on a wetted baking sheet and brush all round the edges with beaten egg. Spread over the apricot conserve.

3 Fold the remaining rectangle in half lengthways and cut about eight diagonal slits from the centre fold to within about 1cm/½ in from the edge all the way along.

4 Unfold the pastry and lay it on t of the conserve covered pastry o the baking sheet. Press the pastry edg together well to seal and knock up with the back of a knife.

5 Brush the slashed pastry with water and sprinkle over the cast sugar and flaked almonds.

6 Bake in the oven for 25–30 minutes, until well risen and golden brown. Remove the jalousie from the oven and leave to cool. Ser sliced, with cream or natural yogurt.

COOK'S TIP

Use other flavours of fruit conserve to fil the jalousie, or, if you prefer, substitute some canned fruit pie filling instead. You could also make smaller, individua jalousies to serve with morning coffee.

Crumbles, Custards and Puddings

Traditional hot desserts are everyone's favourite – classic crumbles filled with summer gooseberries or autumn plums, apples and blackberries, and sponge puddings flavoured with fruit or sticky toffee, are scrumptious family fare. New variations on old favourites include the Apple Couscous Pudding and Chocolate and Orange Soufflés; both are delicious and easy to prepare. When you are entertaining friends, Hot Chocolate Cake makes a divine dessert served with white chocolate sauce, while Caramel Rice Pudding and Poppyseed Custard with Red Fruit are old-fashioned recipes with a new twist. Instead of baking a pie, try plums wrapped in individual crisp filo pockets – they are exceedingly simple to make and can be prepared in advance ready to cook.

Crunchy Gooseberry Crumble

Gooseberries are perfect for traditional family puddings like this one. When they are out of season, other fruits such as apple, plums, or rhubarb could be used instead.

INGREDIENTS 🍎

Serves 4

500g/1¼lb/5 cups gooseberries
50g/2oz/4 tbsp caster sugar
75g/3oz/1 cup rolled oats
75g/3oz/¾ cup wholemeal flour
60ml/4 tbsp sunflower oil
50g/2oz/4 tbsp demerara sugar
30ml/2 tbsp chopped walnuts
natural yogurt or custard, to serve

1 Preheat the oven to 200°C/400°F/ Gas 6. Place the gooseberries in a pan with the caster sugar. Cover the pan and cook over low heat for 10 minutes, until the gooseberries are just tender. Tip into a ovenproof dish.

2 To make the crumble, place the oats, flour, and oil in a bowl and stir with a fork until evenly mixed.

3 Stir in the demerara sugar and walnuts, then spread evenly over the gooseberries. Bake for 25–30 minutes, or until golden and bubbling. Serve hot with yogurt, or custard made with skimmed milk.

--- COOK'S TIP ---

The best cooking gooseberries are the early small, firm green ones.

--- VARIATION ---

If you can't find fresh gooseberries, use either rhubarb or not-too-sweet plums instead. Pecan nuts, almonds or hazelnuts could be substituted for the walnuts, if you prefer.

Pear and Blackberry Brown Betty

[...]l this delicious fruity pudding
[ne]eds to go with it is some hot,
[ho]me-made custard, pouring
[cr]eam or ice cream.

[IN]GREDIENTS

[Se]rves 4–6
[...]g/3oz/6 tbsp butter, diced
[17]5g/6oz/3 cups breadcrumbs made
from one day old bread
[45]0g/1lb ripe pears
[45]0g/1lb blackberries
[gr]ated rind and juice of 1 small orange
[11]5g/4oz/scant ½ cup demerara sugar
[de]merara sugar, for sprinkling

[1] Preheat the oven to 180°C/350°F/
Gas 4. Heat the butter in a heavy
[fry]ing pan over a moderate heat, add
[th]e breadcrumbs and stir until golden.

3 Mix the demerara sugar with the
breadcrumbs, then layer with the
fruit in a 900ml/1½ pint/3 cup buttered
baking dish, beginning and ending
with a layer of sugared breadcrumbs.

4 Sprinkle the extra sugar over the
top. Cover the baking dish, then
bake the pudding for 20 minutes.
Uncover the pudding, then bake for a
further 30–35 minutes, until the fruit is
cooked and the top brown and crisp.

VARIATION

To make Apple and Raspberry Brown
Betty, substitute tart eating apples for the
pears and use fresh, but not too ripe, raspberries in place of the blackberries.

2 Peel and core the pears, then cut
them into thick slices and mix with
[th]e blackberries, orange rind and juice.

Hot Plum Batter Pudding

Other fruits can be used in place of plums, depending on the season. Canned black cherries are also a convenient storecupboard substitute.

INGREDIENTS 🍎

Serves 4
450g/1lb ripe red plums, quartered and stoned
200ml/7fl oz/⅞ cup skimmed milk
60ml/4 tbsp skimmed milk powder
15ml/1 tbsp light muscovado sugar
5ml/1 tsp vanilla essence
75g/3oz self-raising flour
2 egg whites
icing sugar, to sprinkle

1 Preheat the oven to 220°C/425°F/ Gas 7. Lightly oil a wide, shallow ovenproof dish and add the plums.

2 Pour the milk, milk powder, sugar, vanilla, flour, and egg whites into a food processor. Process until smooth.

3 Pour the batter over the plums. Bake for 25–30 minutes, or until puffed and golden. Sprinkle with icing sugar and serve immediately.

COOK'S TIP

If you don't have a food processor, then place the dry ingredients for the batter in a large bowl and gradually whisk in the milk and egg whites.

Glazed Apricot Pudding

Proper puddings are usually very high in saturated fat, but this one uses the minimum of oil and no eggs at all.

INGREDIENTS 🍎

Serves 4
10ml/2 tsp corn syrup
411g/14½oz can apricot halves in fruit juice
150g/5oz/1¼ cup self-raising flour
75g/3oz/1½ cups fresh breadcrumbs
90g/3½oz/⅔ cup light muscovado sugar
5ml/1 tsp ground cinnamon
30ml/2 tbsp sunflower oil
175ml/6fl oz/¾ cup skimmed milk

1 Preheat the oven to 180°C/350°F/ Gas 4. Lightly oil a 900ml/1½ pint/3¾ cup pudding basin. Spoon in the golden syrup.

2 Drain the apricots and reserve the juice. Arrange about eight halves in the basin. Purée the rest of the apricots with the juice and set aside.

3 Mix the flour, breadcrumbs, sugar and cinnamon, then beat in the oil and milk. Spoon into the basin and bake for 50–55 minutes, or until firm and golden. Turn out and serve with the puréed fruit as a sauce.

COOK'S TIP

Make sure that the pudding basin you use is ovenproof. If you don't have one, use another deep ovenproof dish instead – a soufflé dish would be ideal.

Fruity Bread Pudding

A delicious family favourite pud from grandmother's day, with a lighter, healthier touch.

INGREDIENTS 🍎

Serves 4

75g/3oz/⅔ cup mixed dried fruit
150ml/¼ pint/⅔ cup apple juice
115g/4oz stale brown or white
  bread, diced
5ml/1 tsp mixed spice
1 large banana, sliced
150ml/¼ pint/⅔ cup skimmed milk
15ml/1 tbsp demerara sugar
natural low fat yogurt, to serve

1 Preheat the oven to 200°C/400°F/ Gas 6. Place the dried fruit in a small pan with the apple juice and bring to a boil.

2 Remove the pan from the heat and stir in the bread, spice, and banana. Spoon the mixture into a shallow 1.2 litre/2 pint/5 cup ovenproof dish and pour over the milk.

3 Sprinkle with demerara sugar and bake for 25–30 minutes, until firm and golden brown. Serve hot or cold with natural yogurt.

COOK'S TIP
Different types of bread will absorb varying amounts of liquid, so you may need to adjust the milk to allow for this.

VARIATION
To make this pudding extra-special use ready-to-eat dried fruits, such as apricots, dates, figs, mangoes or pears, chopped roughly.

Gingerbread Upside-down Pudding

A proper pudding goes down well on a cold winter's day. This one is quite quick to make and looks very impressive.

INGREDIENTS

Serves 4–6

sunflower oil, for brushing
15ml/1 tbsp soft brown sugar
3 medium peaches, halved and stoned, or canned peach halves
9 walnut halves

For the base

130g/4½oz/½ cup wholemeal flour
2.5ml/½ tsp bicarbonate of soda
7.5ml/1½ tsp ground ginger
5ml/1 tsp ground cinnamon
115g/4oz/½ cup molasses sugar
1 egg
120ml/4fl oz/½ cup skimmed milk
50ml/2fl oz/¼ cup sunflower oil

1 Preheat the oven to 175°C/350°F/ Gas 4. For the topping, brush the base and sides of a 23cm/9in round springform cake tin with oil, Sprinkle the sugar over the base.

2 Arrange the peaches cut-side down in the tin with a walnut half in each.

3 For the base, sift together the flour, bicarbonate of soda, ginger, and cinnamon, then stir in the sugar. Beat together the egg, milk and oil, then mix into the dry ingredients until smooth.

4 Pour the mixture evenly over the peaches and bake for 35–40 minutes, until firm to the touch. Turn out onto a serving plate. Serve hot with yogurt or custard.

COOK'S TIP
To make certain that the fruit topping doesn't stitck to the tin, line the base with a round of non-stick baking paper or lightly oiled greaseproof paper.

Poppyseed Custard with Red Fruit

INGREDIENTS

Serves 6
600ml/1 pint/2½ cups milk
2 eggs
15–30ml/1–2 tbsp caster sugar
1 tbsp poppyseeds
115g/4oz each of strawberries,
   raspberries and blackberries
15–30ml/1–2 tbsp soft light
   brown sugar
50ml/2fl oz/4 tbsp red grape juice

1 Preheat the oven to 150°C/300°F/
Gas 2. Heat the milk until scalding,
but do not boil. Beat the eggs in a
bowl with the caster sugar and
poppyseeds until creamy.

2 Whisk the milk into the egg mixture
until very well blended. Place a buttered soufflé dish in a shallow roasting
tin, half-filled with hot water.

3 Pour the custard into the soufflé
dish and bake for 50–60 minutes
until just set and the top is golden.

4 While the custard is baking, mix
the fruit with the soft brown sug
and fruit juice. Chill until ready to
serve with the warm baked custard.

Caramel Rice Pudding

Traditional puddings are enjoying a
renaissance and here rice pudding is
given a new twist with a crunchy
caramel topping and a refreshing
fruit accompaniment.

INGREDIENTS

Serves 4
50g/2oz/¼ cup short grain
   pudding rice
75ml/5 tbsp demerara sugar
pinch of salt
400g/14oz can evaporated milk made
   up to 600ml/1 pint/2½ cups with
   cold water
knob of butter
1 small fresh pineapple
2 crisp eating apples
10ml/2 tsp lemon juice

1 Preheat the oven to 150°C/300°F/
Gas 2. Put the rice in a sieve and
wash thoroughly under cold water.
Drain well and put into a lightly
greased soufflé dish.

2 Add 30ml/2 tbsp sugar and the salt
to the dish. Pour on the diluted
evaporated milk and stir gently.

3 Dot the surface of the rice with
butter and bake for 2 hours, then
leave to cool for 30 minutes.

4 Meanwhile, peel, core and slice
apples and pineapple, then cut th
pineapple into chunks. Toss the fruit
lemon juice and set aside.

5 Preheat the grill and sprinkle the
remaining sugar over the rice. G
for 5 minutes until the sugar has
caramelised. Leave the rice to stand f
5 minutes to allow the caramel to
harden, then serve with the fresh frui

Baked Apples with Apricots

INGREDIENTS

Serves 4

75g/3oz/scant 1 cup ground almonds
25g/1oz/2 tbsp butter, softened
5ml/1 tsp clear honey
1 egg yolk
50g/2oz/⅓ cup dried apricots, chopped
4 cooking apples, preferably Bramleys

1 Preheat the oven to 200°C/400°F/ Gas 6. Beat together the almonds, butter, honey, egg yolk and apricots.

2 Stamp out the cores from the cooking apples using a large apple corer, then score a line with the point of a sharp knife around the circumference of each apple.

3 Lightly grease a shallow baking dish, then arrange the cooking apples in the dish.

4 Divide the apricot mixture among the cavities in the apples, then bake for 45–60 minutes, until the apples are fluffy.

COOK'S TIP

If cooking apples are unavailable, use four large, tart eating apples.

Kentish Cherry Batter Pudding

Kent, known as the 'Garden of England', has been particularly well-known for cherries and the dishes made from them.

INGREDIENTS

Serves 4

45ml/3 tbsp kirsch (optional)
450g/1lb dark cherries, pitted
50g/2oz/½ cup plain flour
50g/2oz/4 tbsp caster sugar
2 eggs, separated
300ml/½ pint/¼ cups milk
75g/3oz/5 tbsp butter, melted
caster sugar, for sprinkling

1 Sprinkle the kirsch, if using, over the cherries in a small bowl and leave them to soak for about 30 minutes.

2 Mix the flour and sugar together, then slowly stir in the egg yolks and milk to make a smooth batter. Stir in half the butter and leave for 30 minutes.

3 Preheat the oven to 220°C/425°F/ Gas 7. Pour the remaining butter into a 600 ml/1 pint/2½ cup baking dish and put in the oven to heat.

4 Whisk the egg whites until stiff, then fold into the batter with the cherries and kirsch, if using. Pour into the dish and bake for 15 minutes.

5 Reduce the oven temperature to 180°C/350°F/Gas 4 and bake for 20 minutes, or until golden and set in the centre. Serve sprinkled with sugar.

Baked American Cheesecake

INGREDIENTS

Makes 9 squares

For the base

175g/6oz/1½ cups crushed sweetmeal
  biscuits
40g/1½oz/3 tbsp butter, melted

For the topping

450g/1lb/2½ cups curd cheese or
  full fat soft cheese
115g/4oz/½ cup caster sugar
3 eggs
finely grated rind of 1 lemon
15ml/1 tbsp lemon juice
2.5ml/½ tsp vanilla essence
15ml/1 tbsp cornflour
30ml/2 tbsp soured cream
150ml/¼ pint/⅔ cup soured cream and
  1.25ml/¼ tsp ground cinnamon, to
  decorate

1 Preheat the oven to 170°C/325°F/ Gas 3. Lightly grease and line an 18cm/7in square loose-based tin.

2 Place the crushed biscuits and butter in a bowl and mix well. Tip into the base of the prepared cake tin and press down firmly with a potato masher.

3 Place the cheese in a bowl, add t sugar and beat well until smooth Add the eggs one at a time, beating well after each addition and then stir the lemon rind and juice, the vanilla essence, cornflour and soured cream. Beat until smooth.

4 Pour the mixture on to the biscu base and level out. Bake for abou 1¼ hours, or until the cheesecake has set in the centre. Turn off the oven and leave inside until completely col

5 Remove the cheesecake from the top with the soured cream and swi with the back of a spoon. Sprinkle w cinnamon and cut into squares.

Hot Chocolate Cake

his is wonderfully wicked,
her hot as a pudding, to serve
th a white chocolate sauce, or
ld as a cake. The basic cake
ezes well – thaw, then warm in
e microwave before serving.

GREDIENTS

kes 10–12 slices

0g/7oz/1¾ cups self-raising
wholemeal flour
g/1oz/¼ cup cocoa powder
nch of salt
5g/6oz/¾ cup soft margarine
5g/6oz/¾ cup soft light brown sugar
v drops vanilla essence
ggs
g/3oz white chocolate, roughly
hopped
ocolate leaves and curls, to decorate

r the white chocolate sauce

g/3oz white chocolate
0ml/¼ pint/⅔ cup single cream
–40ml/2–3 tbsp milk

1 Preheat the oven to 160°C/325°F/
Gas 3. Sift the flour, cocoa powder
d salt into a bowl, adding back in the
hole wheat flakes from the sieve.

2 Cream the margarine, sugar and
vanilla essence together until light
d fluffy, then gently beat in one egg.

3 Gradually stir in the remaining eggs,
one at a time, alternately folding in
me of the flour, until all the flour
ixture is well blended in.

4 Stir in the white chocolate and
spoon into a 675–900g/1½ –2lb
loaf tin or a 18cm/7in greased cake tin.
Bake for 30–40 minutes, or until just
firm to the touch and shrinking away
from the sides of the pan.

5 Meanwhile, prepare the sauce. Heat
the chocolate and cream very gently
in a pan until the chocolate is melted.
Add the milk and stir until cool.

6 Serve the cake sliced, in a pool of
sauce and decorated with chocolate
leaves and curls.

Sticky Toffee Pudding

INGREDIENTS

Serves 6

115g/4oz/1 cup toasted walnuts,
  chopped
175g/6oz/¾ cup butter
175g/6oz/scant 1 cup soft
  brown sugar
60ml/4 tbsp light cream
30ml/2 tbsp lemon juice
2 eggs, beaten
115g/4oz/1 cup self-raising flour

1 Grease a 900ml/1½ pint pudding
  basin and add half the walnuts.

2 Heat 50g/2oz/4 tbsp of the butter
  with 50g/2oz/4 tbsp of the sugar,
the cream and 15ml/1 tbsp lemon juice
in a small pan, stirring until smooth.
Pour half into the pudding basin, then
swirl to coat it a little way up the sides.

3 Beat the remaining butter and
  sugar until light and fluffy, then
gradually beat in the eggs. Fold in the
flour and the remaining nuts and
lemon juice and spoon into the bowl.

4 Cover the bowl with greaseproof
  paper with a pleat folded in the
centre, then tie securely with string.

5 Steam the pudding for about 1¼
  hours, until set in the centre.

6 Just before serving, gently warm
  the remaining sauce. Unmould
the pudding on to a warm plate and
pour over the warm sauce.

Chocolate and Orange Soufflés

The base in this soufflé is an
easy-to-make semolina mixture,
rather than the thick white sauce
that most soufflés call for.

INGREDIENTS

Serves 4

50g/2oz/generous ⅓ cup semolina
50g/2oz/scant ¼ cup brown sugar
600ml/1 pint/2½ cups milk
grated rind of 1 orange
90ml/6 tbsp fresh orange juice
3 eggs, separated
65g/2½oz plain chocolate,
  grated
icing sugar, for sprinkling

1 Preheat the oven to 200°C/400°F/
  Gas 6. Butter a shallow 1.75 litre/
3 pint/7½ cup ovenproof dish.

2 Pour the milk into a heavy-based
  saucepan, sprinkle over the
semolina and brown sugar, then heat,
stirring the mixture all the time, until
boiling and thickened.

3 Remove the pan from the heat,
  beat in the orange rind and juice,
egg yolks and all but 15ml/1 tbsp of
the grated chocolate.

4 Whisk the egg whites until stiff but
  not dry, then lightly fold into the
semolina mixture in three batches.
Spoon the mixture into the dish and
bake for about 30 minutes, until just set
in the centre and risen. Sprinkle the
top with the reserved chocolate and the
icing sugar, then serve immediately.

Austrian Nut Pudding

INGREDIENTS

Serves 4

butter, for greasing
50g/2oz/4 tbsp caster sugar, plus
  a little extra for sprinkling
115g/4oz/1 cup chopped hazelnuts
50g/2oz/4 tbsp butter, softened
2 eggs, separated
25g/1oz/½ cup very fine fresh white
  breadcrumbs
175g/6oz/1¼ cups fresh raspberries
icing sugar, to taste
cream, to serve

1 Preheat the oven to 160°C/325°F/
Gas 3. Lightly grease a 900ml/
1½ pint/3¾ cup pudding basin and
sprinkle evenly with a little caster sugar.

2 Spread the hazelnuts on to a baking
sheet and bake for 15–20 minutes,
until toasted and golden. Remove from
the oven and leave to cool.

3 Meanwhile, place the butter and
sugar in a bowl and beat until pale
and creamy. Beat in the egg yolks.

4 Process the cooled nuts in a food
processor until finely ground.

5 Mix 15ml/1 tbsp water into the
breadcrumbs and beat into the
creamed mixture with the hazelnuts.

6 Place the egg whites in a clean bowl
and whisk until stiff. Beat about
30ml/2 tbsp into the creamed mixture
to loosen it slightly and carefully fold
the remainder with a metal spoon.

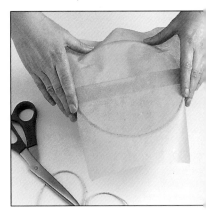

7 Spoon into the prepared basin and
top with a circle of greaseproof
paper with a fold in it, secured tightly
with string. Cover with foil and steam
for 1½ hours, checking and topping up
the water level if it needs it.

8 Meanwhile, press the raspberries
through a sieve into a bowl and
add icing sugar to sweeten. When the
pudding is cooked, turn out and serve
hot with the raspberry sauce and
cream.

Castle Puddings with Custard

GREDIENTS

ves 4

out 45ml/3 tbsp blackcurrant,
trawberry or raspberry jam
5g/4oz/½ cup butter
5g/4oz/generous ½ cup caster
ugar
ggs, beaten
w drops vanilla essence
0g/4½oz/generous cup self-raising
our

r the custard
0ml/¾ pint/scant 1 cup milk
ggs
5–30ml/1½–2 tbsp sugar
w drops vanilla essence

Preheat the oven to 180°C/350°F/
Gas 4. Butter eight dariole moulds.
t about 10ml/2 tsp of the jam in the
e of each mould.

Beat the butter and sugar together
in a bowl until light and fluffy,
n gradually beat in the eggs, beating
ll after each addition and adding the
nilla essence towards the end. Lightly
d in the flour, then divide the
xture among the moulds.

3 Bake the puddings for about 20
minutes, until well risen and a
light golden colour.

4 Meanwhile, make the sauce.
Whisk the eggs and sugar together.
Bring the milk to the boil in a heavy,
preferably non-stick, saucepan, then
slowly pour on to the sweetened egg
mixture, stirring constantly.

5 Return the milk to the pan and heat
very gently, stirring, until the mixture thickens enough to coat the back
of a spoon; do not allow to boil. Cover
the pan and remove from the heat.

6 Remove from the oven, leave to
stand for a few minutes, then turn
the puddings on to warmed plates and
serve with the custard.

COOK'S TIP

Instead of baking the puddings, you can
steam them for 30–40 minutes. If you do
not have dariole moulds, use ramekins
instead.

Zabaglione

A much-loved Italian dessert traditionally made with Marsala. Madeira is a good alternative.

INGREDIENTS

Serves 4
4 egg yolks
50g/2oz/4 tbsp caster sugar
60ml/4 tbsp Marsala or Madeira wine
amaretti biscuits, to serve

1 Place the egg yolks and sugar in a large heatproof bowl and whisk with an electric whisk until the mixture is pale and thick.

2 Gradually add the Marsala or Madeira, whisking well after each addition (at this stage the mixture will be quite runny).

3 Now place the bowl over a pan of gently simmering water and continue to whisk for at least 5–7 minutes, until the mixture becomes thick and mousse-like; when the beaters are lifted they should leave a thick trail on the surface of the mixture. (If you don't beat the mixture for long enough, the zabaglione will be too runny and will probably separate.)

4 Pour into four warmed, stemmed glasses and serve immediately with the amaretti biscuits for dipping.

COOK'S TIP

If you don't have any Marsala or Madeira you could use either a medium sherry or a dessert wine.

Mixed Berry Soufflé Omelette

These light French omelettes take only a few minutes to cook and are best eaten straight away.

INGREDIENTS

Makes 2 (serves 4)
4 eggs, separated
finely grated rind of 1 lemon
25g/1oz/2 tbsp caster sugar
drop of vanilla essence
15ml/1 tbsp single cream
25g/1oz/2 tbsp butter
60ml/4 tbsp mixed berry conserve, warmed
icing sugar, for dusting
30ml/2 tbsp toasted flaked almonds and fresh mint sprigs, to decorate

1 Place the egg yolks in a bowl and add the lemon rind, sugar, vanilla essence and cream. Beat with an electric or balloon whisk until pale and slightly thickened, then set aside.

2 Whisk the egg whites in a separate bowl until holding stiff peaks. Gently beat 30ml/2 tbsp of the whisked whites into the egg yolk mixture to loosen it, then fold in the remainder using a large metal spoon.

3 Melt half the butter in a 23cm/9in frying pan and pour on half the egg mixture. Cook on a gentle heat for about 4 minutes, or until just set and lightly golden underneath.

4 Pop the pan under the hot grill for about 30 seconds, keeping a close eye on it, until just browned. Remove from the grill, then spoon half the warmed conserve over the omelette. Fold the omelette in half and slide it to a warmed plate.

5 Dust with a little icing sugar, sprinkle with half the almonds and decorate with mint. Cut in half and share between two people. Use the remaining mixture to make a second omelette.

Plum and Walnut Crumble

Walnuts add a lovely crunch to the fruit layer in this crumble – almonds would be equally good.

INGREDIENTS

Serves 4–6
75g/3oz/¾ cup walnut pieces
75g/3oz/6 tbsp butter or hard margarine, diced
175g/6oz/1½ cups plain flour
175g/6oz/scant 1 cup demerara sugar
1kg/2lb plums, halved and stoned

1 Preheat the oven to 180°C/350°F/ Gas 4. Spread the nuts on a baking sheet and place in the oven for 8–10 minutes, until evenly coloured.

2 Butter a 1.2 litre/2 pint/5 cup baking dish. Put the plums into the dish and stir in the nuts and half of the demerara sugar.

3 Rub the butter or margarine into the flour until the mixture resembles coarse crumbs. Stir in the remaining sugar and continue to rub in until fine crumbs are formed.

4 Cover the fruit with the crumb mixture and press it down lightly. Bake the pudding for about 45 minutes, until the top is golden brown and the fruit tender.

--- VARIATION ---

To make Oat and Cinnamon Crumble, substitute rolled oats for half the flour in the crumble mixture and add 2.5– 5ml/½–1 tsp ground cinnamon.

Rhubarb and Strawberry Crisp

NGREDIENTS

erves 4

25g/8oz strawberries, hulled and cut
 in half if large
50g/1lb rhubarb, cut into pieces
0g/3½oz/½ cup caster sugar
5ml/1 tbsp cornstarch
5ml/3fl oz/⅓ cup fresh orange juice
15g/4oz/1 cup plain flour
5g/3oz/1 cup rolled oats
0g/3½oz/½ cup light brown sugar
.5ml/½ tsp ground cinnamon
0g/1½oz/½ cup ground almonds
50g/5oz/10 tbsp cold butter
 egg, lightly beaten

1 Preheat the oven to 180°C/350°F/
Gas 4, then mix together the
rawberries, rhubarb and sugar in a
.75 litre/3 pint/7½ cup baking dish.

2 Blend the cornflour with the
orange juice in a small bowl, then
our this mixture over the fruit and
tir gently to coat. Set the baking dish
side while making the topping.

3 Toss together the flour, oats,
brown sugar, cinnamon and
almonds in a large bowl. Rub in the
butter using your fingertips until the
mixture resembles coarse breadcrumbs,
then stir in the beaten egg.

4 Spoon the oat mixture evenly over
the fruit and press down gently.
Bake for about 50–60 minutes, until
browned. Serve the crumble warm.

Plum Filo Pockets

INGREDIENTS 🍎

Serves 4

115g/4oz/½ cup skimmed milk soft
   cheese
15ml/1 tbsp light muscovado sugar
2.5ml/½ tsp ground cloves
8 large, firm plums, halved and stoned
8 sheets filo pastry
sunflower oil, for brushing
icing sugar, to sprinkle

1 Preheat the oven to 220°C/425°F/
Gas 7. Mix together the cheese,
sugar, and cloves.

2 Sandwich the plum halves back
together in twos with a spoonful of
the cheese mixture.

3 Spread out the pastry and cut into
16 pieces, each about 23cm/9in
square. Brush one lightly with oil and
place a second at a diagonal on top.
Repeat with the remaining pastry to
make eight double-layer squares.

4 Place a plum on each pastry square
and pinch corners together. Place o
baking sheet. Bake for 15–18 minutes,
until golden, then dust with icing sugar

--- VARIATION ---

In the summer, you could use large fresh
apricots, or small peaches or nectarines in
place of the plums – make sure that the
fruit is just ripe.

Apple Couscous Pudding

This unusual couscous mixture
makes a delicious family pudding
with a rich fruity flavour, but
virtually no fat.

INGREDIENTS 🍎

Serves 4

600ml/2 pint/2½ cups apple juice
115g/4oz/⅔ cup couscous
40g/1½oz/¼ cup sultanas
2.5ml/½ tsp mixed spice
1 large Bramley cooking apple, peeled,
   cored, and sliced
2 tbsp demerara sugar
natural low fat yogurt, to serve

1 Preheat the oven to 200°C/400°F/
Gas 6. Place the apple juice,
couscous, sultanas and spice in a pan
and bring to the boil, stirring. Cover
and simmer for 10–12 minutes, until all
the free liquid is absorbed.

2 Spoon half the couscous mixture
into a 1.2 litre/2 pint/5 cup ovenproof dish and top with half the apple
slices. Top with the remaining couscous.

3 Arrange the remaining apple slice
overlapping over the top and
sprinkle with demerara sugar. Bake fo
25–30 minutes, or until golden brown
Serve hot with yogurt.

--- COOK'S TIP ---

To ring the changes, substitute other dried
fruits for the sultanas in this recipe – try
chopped dates or ready-to-eat pears, figs
or apricots.

Cold Desserts and Ices

Chilled desserts not only look wonderful, they have the added advantage of being prepared in advance, so recipes such as Lemon Soufflé with Blackberries, Rose Petal Cream, and Ginger and Orange Crème Brûlée are ideal to make when you are entertaining. Meringues are perfect for parties and can be cooked a week or two before you need them, then filled just before serving – there are three gorgeous recipes to choose from. Preparing ahead is a boon for everyday meals too, and Tangerine Trifle and Crème Caramel are both delicious family treats. Ice creams and frozen desserts will keep perfectly in the freezer for weeks, if not months – simple ice creams flavoured with mango, toasted breadcrumbs or flakes of chocolate will delight your family, while Strawberry Mousse Cake and Iced Chocolate and Nut Gâteau are perfect desserts to have on hand for unexpected guests.

Almost Instant Banana Pudding

INGREDIENTS

Serves 6–8

4 thick slices ginger cake
6 bananas, sliced
30ml/2 tbsp lemon juice
300ml/½ pint/1¼ cups whipping
  cream or fromage frais
60ml/4 tbsp fruit juice
30–45ml/3–4 tbsp soft brown sugar

1 Break up the cake into chunks and arrange in an ovenproof dish. Slice the bananas and toss in the lemon juice.

2 Whip the cream and, when firm, gently whip in the juice. (If using fromage frais, just gently stir in the juice.) Fold in the bananas and spoon the mixture over the ginger cake.

3 Top with the sugar and place under a hot grill for 2–3 minutes to caramelise. Chill to set firm again i you wish, or serve when required.

Ginger and Orange Crème Brûlée

This is a useful way of cheating at crème brûlée! Most people would never know unless you overchill the custard, or keep it more than a day, but there's little risk of that!

INGREDIENTS

Serves 4–5

2 eggs, plus 2 egg yolks
300ml/½ pint/1¼ cups single cream
25g/1oz/2 tbsp caster sugar
5ml/1 tsp powdered gelatine
finely grated rind and juice of ½ orange
1 large piece stem ginger, finely
  chopped
45–60ml/3–4 tbsp icing or caster
  sugar

1 Whisk the eggs and yolks together until pale. Bring the cream and sugar to the boil, remove from the heat and sprinkle on the gelatine. Stir until the gelatine has dissolved and then pour the cream mixture onto the eggs, whisking all the time.

2 Add the orange rind, a little juice to taste, and the chopped ginger.

3 Pour into 4 or 5 ramekins and chill until set.

4 Some time before serving, sprink the sugar generously over the top of the custard and put under a very h grill. Watch closely for the couple of moments it takes for the tops to caramelise. Allow to cool before servin

—— COOK'S TIP ——

For a milder ginger flavour, just add up to 5ml/1 tsp ground ginger instead of the stem ginger.

Frozen Strawberry Mousse Cake

Children love this dessert – it is pink and pretty, and tastes just like an ice cream.

INGREDIENTS
Serves 4–6

425g/15oz can strawberries in syrup
15ml/1 tbsp/1 sachet powdered
  gelatine
6 trifle sponge cakes
45ml/3 tbsp strawberry conserve
200ml/7fl oz/⅞ cup crème fraîche
200ml/7fl oz/⅞ cup whipped cream,
  to decorate

1 Strain the syrup from the strawberries into a large heatproof bowl. Sprinkle over the gelatine and stir well. Stand the bowl in a pan of hot water and stir until the gelatine has dissolved.

2 Leave to cool, then chill for just under 1 hour, until beginning to set. Meanwhile, cut the sponge cakes in half lengthways and spread the cut surfaces with the strawberry conserve.

3 Slowly whisk the crème fraîche into the strawberry jelly, then whisk in the canned strawberries. Line a deep, 20cm/8in loose-based cake tin with non-stick baking paper.

4 Pour half the strawberry mousse mixture into the tin, arrange the sponge cakes over the surface, and the spoon over the remaining mousse mixture, pushing down any sponge cakes which rise up.

5 Freeze for 1–2 hours until firm. Unmould the cake and carefully remove the lining paper. Transfer to a serving plate. Decorate with whirls of cream and a few strawberry leaves and a fresh strawberry, if you have them.

Lemon Soufflé with Blackberries

e simple fresh taste of the cold
1on mousse combines well with
: rich blackberry sauce, and the
our contrast looks wonderful,
). Blueberries or raspberries make
1ally delicious alternatives to
ckberries.

GREDIENTS
ves 6
ted rind of 1 lemon and juice
f 2 lemons
ml/1 tbsp/1 sachet powdered
elatine
ze 4 eggs, separated
)g/5oz/10 tbsp caster sugar
v drops vanilla essence
)ml/14fl oz/1²⁄₃ cups whipping cream

r the sauce
5g/6oz blackberries (fresh or frozen)
-45ml/2–3 tbsp caster sugar
v fresh blackberries and blackberry
:aves, to decorate

Place the lemon juice in a small
pan and heat through. Sprinkle on
gelatine and leave to dissolve or
t further until clear. Allow to cool.

2 Put the lemon rind, egg yolks,
sugar and vanilla into a large bowl
and whisk until the mixture is very
thick, pale and creamy.

3 Whisk the egg whites until stiff
and almost peaky. Whip the cream
until stiff and holding its shape.

4 Stir the gelatine mixture into the
yolks, then fold in the whipped
cream and lastly the egg whites. When
lightly but thoroughly blended, turn
into a 1.5 litre/2½ pint/6 cup soufflé
dish and freeze for about 2 hours.

5 To make the sauce, place the blackberries in a pan with the sugar and
cook for 4–6 minutes, until the juices
begin to run and all the sugar has dissolved. Pass through a sieve to remove
the seeds, then chill until ready to serve.

6 When the soufflé is almost frozen,
but still spoonable, scoop or spoon
out on to individual plates and serve
with the blackberry sauce.

Raspberry Meringue Gâteau

A rich, hazelnut meringue filled with cream and raspberries makes a wonderful dessert.

INGREDIENTS

Serves 6
4 egg whites
225g/8oz/1 cup caster sugar
few drops vanilla essence
5ml/1 tsp distilled malt vinegar
115g/4oz/1 cup roasted and chopped
  hazelnuts, ground
300ml/½ pint/1¼ cups double cream
350g/12oz raspberries
icing sugar, for dusting
raspberries and mint sprigs,
  to decorate

For the sauce
225g/8oz raspberries
45–60ml/3–4 tbsp icing sugar, sifted
15ml/1 tbsp orange liqueur

1 Preheat the oven to 180°C/350°F/ Gas 4. Grease two 20cm/8in sandwich tins and line the bases with greaseproof paper.

2 Whisk the egg whites in a large bowl until they hold stiff peaks, then gradually whisk in the caster sugar a tablespoon at a time, whisking well after each addition.

3 Continue whisking the meringue mixture for a minute or two until very stiff, then fold in the vanilla essence, vinegar and ground hazelnuts.

4 Divide the meringue mixture between the prepared sandwich tins and spread level. Bake for 50–60 minutes, until crisp. Remove the meringues from the tins and leave to cool on a wire rack.

5 While the meringues are cooling, make the sauce. Purée the raspberries with the icing sugar and orange liqueur in a blender or food processor, then press the purée through a fine nylon sieve to remove any pips. Chill the sauce until ready to serve.

COOK'S TIP

You can buy roasted chopped hazelnuts in supermarkets. Otherwise toast whole hazelnuts under the broiler and rub off the flaky skins using a clean dish towel. To chop finely, whizz in a food processor for a few moments.

6 Whip the cream until it forms s[o] peaks, then gently fold in the ra[sp]berries. Sandwich the meringue rou[nd] together with the raspberry cream.

7 Dust the top of the gâteau with icing sugar. Decorate with raspberries and mint sprigs and serve with the raspberry sauce.

VARIATION

Fresh redcurrants make a good alternativ[e] to raspberries. Pick over the fruit, the[n] pull each sprig gently through the prong[s] of a fork to release the redcurrants. Ad[d] them to the whipped cream with a littl[e] icing sugar, to taste.

Pineapple and Strawberry Pavlova

This is a gooey pavlova which doesn't usually hold a perfect shape, but it has a wonderful mallowy texture.

INGREDIENTS

Serves 6

5 egg whites, at room temperature
pinch of salt
5ml/1 tsp cornstarch
15ml/1 tbsp vinegar
few drops vanilla essence
275g/10oz/1½ cups caster sugar
250ml/8fl oz/1 cup whipping cream, whipped
175g/6oz fresh pineapple, cut into chunks
175g/6oz fresh strawberries, halved
strawberry leaves, to decorate

1 Preheat the oven to 160°C/325°F/ Gas 3. Line a baking sheet with or non-stick baking paper.

2 Put the egg whites in a large bowl and whisk until holding stiff peaks. Add the salt, cornflour, vinegar and vanilla essence; whisk again until stiff.

3 Gently whisk in half the sugar, th carefully fold in the rest. Spoon th meringue on to the baking sheet and swirl into an 20cm/8in round with th back of a large spoon.

4 Bake the meringue for 20 minute then reduce the oven temperature to 150°C/300°F/Gas 2 and bake for a further 40 minutes until the meringue is crisp and dry.

5 Transfer to a serving plate while still warm, then leave to cool. When ready to serve, fill with whippe cream, chunks of pineapple and halve strawberries and decorate with strawberry leaves, if you have them.

— COOK'S TIP —

You can also cook this in a deep, 20cm/8in loose-based cake tin. Cover the base with non-stick baking paper and grease the sides.

Blackberry Brown Sugar Meringue

INGREDIENTS

Serves 6

175g/6oz/1 cup light brown sugar
4 egg whites
5ml/1 tsp distilled malt vinegar
2.5ml/½ tsp vanilla essence

For the filling
350–450g/12oz–1lb blackberries
30ml/2 tbsp crème de cassis
300ml/½ pint/1¼ cups double cream
15ml/1 tbsp icing sugar, sifted
small blackberry leaves, to decorate
(optional)

1 Preheat the oven to 160°C/325°F/
Gas 3. Draw an 20cm/8in circle
on a sheet of non-stick baking paper,
turn over and place on a baking sheet.

2 Spread out the brown sugar on a
baking sheet and dry in the oven for
10 minutes. Sieve to remove lumps.

3 Whisk the egg whites in a bowl
until stiff. Add half the dried
brown sugar, 15ml/1 tbsp at a time,
whisking well after each addition. Add
the vinegar and vanilla essence, then
fold in the remaining sugar.

4 Spoon the meringue on to the
drawn circle on the paper, leaving
a hollow in the centre. Bake for 45
minutes, then turn off the oven and
leave the meringue in the oven with
the door slightly open, until cold.

5 Place the blackberries in a bowl,
sprinkle over the crème de cassis
and leave to macerate for 30 minutes.

6 When the meringue is cold,
carefully peel off the non-stick
baking paper and transfer the meringue to
a serving plate. Lightly whip the cream
with the icing sugar and spoon into the
centre. Top with the blackberries and
decorate with small blackberry leaves, if
liked. Serve at once.

Chocolate Flake Ice Cream

It doesn't matter whether or not you have an ice cream machine for this recipe – it's so quick, and just needs occasional whisking. Either bitter chocolate biscuits or a hot apricot sauce would be a delicious accompaniment.

INGREDIENTS

Serves 6

300ml/½ pint/1¼ cups whipping cream, chilled
90ml/6 tbsp Greek-style yogurt
75–90ml/5–6 tbsp caster sugar
few drops vanilla essence
150g/5oz/10 tbsp flaked or roughly grated chocolate

1 Have ready a 600–900ml/1–1½ pint/3–4 cup freezer container, preferably with a lid. Prepare a place in the freezer so you can easily reach it.

2 Softly whip the cream in a large bowl and fold in the yogurt, sugar, vanilla essence and chocolate. Stir gently to mix thoroughly and then transfer to the freezer container.

3 Smooth the top of the ice cream then cover and freeze. Gently stir with a fork every half hour or so, until it is too hard to stir – this may take up to 4 hours. Serve in scoops.

Mango and Raspberry Fool

INGREDIENTS

Serves 4–6

1 ripe mango
15ml/1 tbsp lemon juice
225g/8oz raspberries, fresh, or frozen and defrosted
caster sugar, to taste
2 egg whites
150ml/¼ pint/⅔ cup whipping cream

2 Set aside a few raspberries for decoration. Add the remainder to the mango and purée in a food processor until smooth. Press through a sieve into a large bowl and sweeten to taste.

3 Whisk the egg whites stiffly and whip the cream into soft peaks. Fold them both gently into the fruit purée. When well blended, spoon into glasses and chill. Serve decorated with the reserved raspberries.

COOK'S TIP

When fresh mangoes are not available, use two large ripe peaches or nectarines, or about 225g/8oz fresh, ripe apricots.

1 Peel the mango and then cut the flesh away from the central stone and place in a bowl. Sprinkle over the lemon juice.

Iced Chocolate and Nut Gâteau

Autumn hazelnuts add crunchiness to this delicious iced dessert.

INGREDIENTS

Serves 6–8
75g/3oz/½ cup shelled hazelnuts
about 32 sponge fingers
150ml/¼ pint/⅔ cup cold strong
  black coffee
30ml/2 tbsp brandy
450ml/¾ pint/1⅞ cups double cream
75g/3oz/6 tbsp icing sugar, sifted
150g/5oz plain chocolate
icing sugar and cocoa, for dusting

1 Preheat the oven to 200°C/400°F/ Gas 6. Spread out the hazelnuts on a baking sheet and toast them in the oven for 5 minutes until golden.

2 Transfer the nuts to a clean dish towel and rub off the skins while still warm. Cool, then chop finely.

3 Line a 1.2 litre/2 pint/5 cup loaf tin with clear film and cut the sponge fingers to fit the base and sides. Reserve the remaining biscuits.

4 Mix the coffee with the brandy in a shallow dish. Dip the sponge fingers briefly into the coffee mixture and return to the tin, sugary side down.

5 Whip the cream with the icing sugar until it holds soft peaks. Roughly chop 75g/3oz of the chocolate, and fold into the cream with the hazelnuts.

6 Melt the remaining chocolate in a bowl set over a pan of barely simmering water. Cool, then fold into the cream mixture. Spoon into the tin.

7 Moisten the remaining biscuits in the coffee mixture and lay over the filling. Wrap and freeze until firm.

8 To serve, remove from the freezer 30 minutes before serving. Turn out on to a serving plate and dust with icing sugar and cocoa.

Tangerine Trifle

unusual variation on a tradi-
nal trifle – of course, you can
d a little alcohol if you wish.

GREDIENTS

ves 4

rifle sponges, halved lengthways
ml/2 tbsp apricot conserve
–20 ratafia biscuits
2g/4¾oz packet tangerine jelly
0g/11oz can mandarin oranges,
drained, reserving juice
0ml/1 pint/2½ cups ready-made (or
home-made) custard
nipped cream and shreds of orange
ind, to decorate
ter sugar, for sprinkling

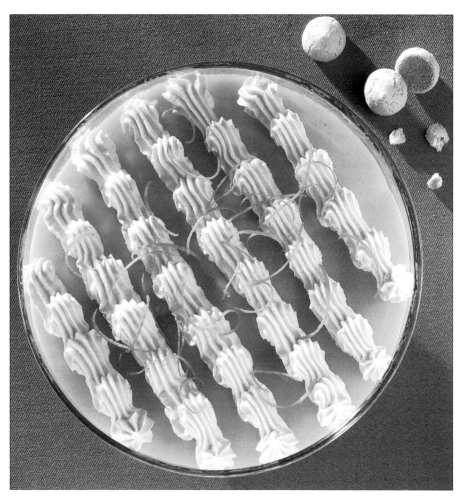

Spread the halved sponge cakes
with apricot conserve and arrange
the base of a deep serving bowl or
ss dish. Sprinkle over the ratafia.

Break up the jelly into a heatproof
measuring jug, add the juice from
e canned mandarins and dissolve in a
n of hot water or in the microwave.
r until the liquid clears.

3 Make up to 600ml/1 pint/2½ cups
with ice cold water, stir well and
leave to cool for up to 30 minutes.
Scatter the mandarin oranges over the
cakes and ratafias.

4 Pour the jelly over the mandarin
oranges, cake and ratafias and chill
for 1 hour, or more.

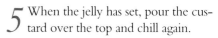

5 When the jelly has set, pour the custard over the top and chill again.

6 When ready to serve, pipe the
whipped cream over the custard.
Wash the orange rind shreds, sprinkle
them with caster sugar and use to
decorate the trifle.

Crème Caramel

The classic, creamy, caramel-flavoured custard from France.

INGREDIENTS

Serves 4–6
115g/4oz/½ cup granulated sugar
300ml/½ pint/1¼ cups milk
300ml/½ pint/1¼ cups single cream
6 eggs
75g/3oz/6 tbsp caster sugar
2.5ml/½ tsp vanilla essence

1 Preheat the oven to 150°C/300°F/Gas 2 and half-fill a large roasting tin with water.

2 Place the granulated sugar in a saucepan with 60ml/4 tbsp water and heat gently, swirling the pan occasionally, until the sugar has dissolved. Increase the heat and boil, to a good caramel colour.

3 Immediately pour the caramel into an ovenproof soufflé dish. Place in the roasting tin and set aside.

4 To make the egg custard, heat the milk and cream together in a pan until almost boiling. Meanwhile, beat the eggs, caster sugar and vanilla essence together in a bowl using a large balloon whisk.

5 Whisk the hot milk into the eggs and sugar, then strain the liquid through a sieve into the soufflé dish, on top of the cooled caramel base.

6 Transfer the tin to the oven and bake in the centre for about 1½ hours (topping up the water level after 1 hour), or until the custard has set in the centre. Lift the dish carefully out of the water and leave to cool, then cover and chill overnight.

7 Loosen the sides of the chilled custard with a knife and then place an inverted plate (large enough to hold the caramel sauce that will flow out as well) on top of the dish. Holding the dish and plate together, turn upside down and give the whole thing a quick shake to release the crème caramel.

Brown Bread Ice Cream

INGREDIENTS

Serves 6

50g/2oz/½ cup roasted and chopped
  hazelnuts, ground
75g/3oz/1⅓ cups wholemeal
  breadcrumbs
50g/2oz/4 tbsp demerara sugar
3 egg whites
115g/4oz/½ cup caster sugar
300ml/½ pint/1¼ cups double cream
few drops vanilla essence

For the sauce
225g/8oz blackcurrants
75g/3oz/6 tbsp caster sugar
15ml/1 tbsp crème de cassis
fresh mint sprigs, to decorate

1 Combine the hazelnuts and breadcrumbs on a baking sheet, then
sprinkle over the demerara sugar. Place
under a medium grill and cook, stirring,
until the mixture is crisp and evenly
browned. Leave to cool.

2 Whisk the egg whites in a bowl
until stiff, then gradually whisk in
the sugar until thick and glossy. Whip
the cream until it forms soft peaks and
fold into the meringue with the bread-
crumb mixture and vanilla essence.

3 Spoon the mixture into a 1.2 litre/
2 pint/5 cup loaf tin. Smooth the
top level, then cover and freeze for
several hours, or until firm.

4 Meanwhile, make the sauce. Strip
the blackcurrants from their stalks
using a fork and put the blackcurrants
in a small bowl with the sugar. Toss
gently to mix and leave for 30 minutes.

5 Purée the blackcurrants in a blender
or food processor, then press
through a nylon sieve until smooth. Add
the crème de cassis and chill well.

6 To serve, turn out the ice cream
on to a plate and cut into slices.
Arrange each slice on a serving plate,
spoon over a little sauce and decorate
with fresh mint sprigs.

Cherry Syllabub

This recipe follows the style of the earliest syllabubs from the sixteenth and seventeenth centuries, producing a frothy creamy layer over a liquid one.

INGREDIENTS

Serves 4
225g/8oz ripe dark cherries, stoned
  and chopped
30ml/2 tbsp kirsch
2 egg whites
75g/3oz/generous ½ cup caster sugar
30ml/2 tbsp lemon juice
150ml/¼ pint/⅔ cup sweet white wine
300ml/½ pint/1¼ cups double cream

1 Divide the chopped cherries among six tall dessert glasses and sprinkle over the kirsch.

2 In a clean bowl, whisk the egg whites until stiff. Gently fold in the sugar, lemon juice and wine.

3 In a separate bowl (but using the same whisk), lightly beat the cream then fold into the egg white mixture.

4 Spoon the cream mixture over the cherries, then chill overnight.

Rose Petal Cream

This is an old-fashioned junket which is set with rennet – don't move it while it is setting, otherwise it will separate.

INGREDIENTS

Serves 4
600ml/1 pint/2½ cups milk
45ml/3 tbsp caster sugar
several drops triple-strength
  rosewater
10ml/2 tsp rennet
60ml/4 tbsp double cream
sugared rose petals, to decorate
  (optional)

1 Gently heat the milk and 30ml/ 2 tbsp of the sugar, stirring, until the sugar has melted and the temperature reaches 36.9°C/98.4°F, or the milk feels neither hot nor cold.

2 Stir rosewater to taste into the milk, then remove the pan from the heat and stir in the rennet.

3 Pour the milk into a serving dish and leave undisturbed for 2–3 hours, until the junket has set.

4 Stir the remaining sugar into the cream, then carefully spoon over the junket. Decorate with sugared rose petals, if you like.

Apple and Hazelnut Shortcake

INGREDIENTS

Serves 8–10

150g/5oz/1 cup wholemeal flour
50g/2oz/4 tbsp ground hazelnuts
50g/2oz/4 tbsp icing sugar, sifted
150g/5oz/10 tbsp unsalted butter or
   margarine
3 sharp eating apples
5ml/1 tsp lemon juice
15–30ml/1–2 tbsp caster sugar,
   or to taste
15ml/1 tbsp chopped fresh mint,
   or 5ml/1 tsp dried
250ml/8fl oz/1 cup whipping cream
   or crème fraîche
few drops vanilla essence
few mint leaves and whole hazelnuts,
   to decorate

1 Process the flour, ground hazelnuts and icing sugar with the butter in a food processor in short bursts, or rub the butter into the dry ingredients until they come together. (Don't overwork the mixture.) Bring the dough together, adding a very little iced water if necessary. Knead briefly, wrap in greaseproof paper and chill for 30 minutes.

2 Preheat the oven to 160°C/325°F/ Gas 3. Cut the dough in half and roll out each half, on a lightly floured surface, to a 18cm/7in round. Place on greaseproof paper on baking sheets and bake for about 40 minutes, or until crisp. If browning too much, move them down in the oven to a lower shelf. Allow to cool.

3 Peel, core and chop the apples into a pan with the lemon juice. Add sugar to taste, then cook for about 2–3 minutes, until just softening. Mash the apple gently with the chopped fresh mint and leave to cool.

4 Whip the cream with the vanilla essence. Place one shortbread base on a serving plate. Spread half the apple and half the cream or crème fraîche on top.

5 Place the second shortcake on top, then spread over the remaining apple and cream, swirling the top layer of cream gently. Decorate the top with mint leaves and a few whole hazelnuts, then serve at once.

Mango Ice Cream

Mangoes are used widely in Far Eastern cooking, particularly in Thailand, where they are used to make this delicious ice cream.

INGREDIENTS

Serves 4–6

2 x 425g/15oz cans sliced mango, drained
50g/2oz/4 tbsp caster sugar
30ml/2 tbsp lime juice
15ml/1 tbsp powdered gelatine
350ml/12fl oz/1½ cups double cream, lightly whipped
fresh mint sprigs, to decorate

1 Reserve four slices of mango for decoration and chop the remainder. Place the mangoes in a bowl with the sugar and lime juice.

2 Put 45ml/3 tbsp hot water in a small bowl and sprinkle over the gelatine. Place over a pot of gently simmering water and stir until dissolved. Pour on to the mangoes and mix well.

3 Add the lightly whipped cream and fold into the mango mixture. Pour the mixture into a polythene freezer container and freeze until half frozen.

4 Place in a food processor or blender and blend until smooth. Spoon back into the plastic container and re-freeze.

5 Remove from the freezer 10 minutes before serving and place in the fridge. Serve scoops of ice cream decorated with pieces of the reserved sliced mango and fresh mint sprigs.

Raspberry and Cranberry Jelly

INGREDIENTS

Serves 6–8

142g/4¾ oz packet raspberry jelly
250ml/8fl oz/1 cup raspberry and
　cranberry juice
115g/4oz fresh strawberries
115g/4oz raspberries (fresh or
　frozen)
1 large red-skinned apple, cored and
　chopped

1 Break up the jelly into a heatproof
measuring jug and pour on 150ml/¼
pint/⅔ cup boiling water. Stir until dissolved. Then pour in the raspberry and
cranberry juice and leave until setting.

2 Halve or quarter the strawberries,
depending on their size. If using
frozen raspberries, leave them in the
freezer until you put the jelly to set.
Prepare the apple at the last moment.

3 Have ready a pretty 1.2 litre/2
pint/5 cup mould, rinsed out wit
cold water. When the jelly is beginni
to thicken, stir in the fruits. (With
frozen raspberries it will set almost
immediately, so work quickly.) Spoo
into the mould and chill until set.

4 Turn out the jelly on to a servin
plate and serve with custard,
fromage frais or frozen yogurt ice.

Blackberry and Apple Romanoff

Rich yet fruity, this dessert is
popular with most people and
very quick to make.

INGREDIENTS

Serves 6–8

350g/12oz (3–4) sharp eating apples,
　peeled, cored and chopped
45ml/3 tbsp caster sugar
250ml/8fl oz/1 cup whipping cream
5ml/1 tsp grated lemon rind
90ml/6 tbsp Greek-style yogurt
50g/2oz (4–6) crisp meringues,
　roughly crumbled
225g/8oz blackberries (fresh or frozen)
whipped cream, a few blackberries and
　mint leaves, to decorate

1 Line a 900ml/1.2 litre/1½–2
pint/4–5 cup pudding basin with
clear film. Toss the apples into a pan
with 30ml/2 tbsp sugar and cook for
2–3 minutes, or until softening. Mash
with a fork and leave to cool.

2 Whip the cream and fold in the
lemon rind, yogurt, the remaining
sugar, the apples and meringues.

3 Gently stir in the blackberries, the
tip the mixture into the pudding
basin and freeze for 1–3 hours.

4 Turn out on to a plate and remov
the clear film. Decorate with
whirls of cream, blackberries and min

— VARIATION —

This also makes a delicious ice cream,
though the texture of the frozen berries
makes it difficult to scoop if it is frozen for
more than 4–6 hours.

INDEX